VINTAGE
SHOES

THIS IS A CARLTON BOOK

Design and special photography copyright © Carlton Books
      Limited 2008
Text © Caroline Cox 2008
Foreword © Christian Louboutin 2008

This edition published in 2012
by Carlton Books Limited
20 Mortimer Street
London W1T 3JW

10 9 8 7 6 5 4 3 2 1

A CIP catalogue record for this book is available
from the British Library.
ISBN 978 1 78097 160 5
Printed and bound in Dubai

Senior Executive Editor: Lisa Dyer
Managing Art Director: Lucy Coley
Designer: Emma Wicks
Illustrations: Adam Wright
Copy Editor: Jenny McIntyre
Picture Researcher: Jenny Meredith
Production: Janette Burgin
Special Photography: Russell Porter

CAPTIONS: Overleaf, a
pair of Miu Miu shoes
from 2001; this page,
white buckled sandals,
photographed by Norman
Parkinson, 1966; page
4, satin court shoes and
stockings, photographed
by John Rawlings in 1948.

VINTAGE
SHOES

Caroline Cox

CARLTON

Contents

Foreword by Christian Louboutin   6

Introduction   8

1900–19: Edwardian Elegance   10

1920s: The Modernist Shoe   30

1930–47: The Hollywood Heel   56

1948–59: New Look Shoes   88

1960s: A Youth Revolution   114

1970s: Biba and Beyond   146

1980s: Dress for Success   172

1990s to Now: Future Collectables   194

Shopping and Collecting   210

Glossary of Designers   216

Index   219

Further Reading and Acknowledgements   223

Foreword

When you are a child, adults, especially teachers, are always asking you, 'What are you going to do when you grow up?' I was pretty lazy and got so bored with this question I made up an answer, 'A shoe designer.' I had no idea that this was a real job but people began to think I was obsessed with shoes and started giving me any information about it. One day someone gave me a book about a Roger Vivier exhibition and I realized shoe design could be a really beautiful job. Vivier's shoes spoke by themselves – he understood that a shoe has a bone structure and that bone structure has to be perfect. He covers his shoes with beautiful embroidery and embellishment but underneath it all is a perfect plain pump with perfect proportions – pure perfection.

For me, there are two ways of approaching shoe design; you can create a shoe that becomes a small moment in time or you can work in a deeper way with a more personal and perennial perspective like Vivier. Quick consumerist design is not my thing, it's not the way I think. I'm not obsessed with doing something first. When it's ready, it's ready; if not you'll all just have to wait because the process can take years and time is on my side! My priority has always been to create things of beauty. For me, shoes are like pieces of jewellery that only the craziest woman would want to throw away. It gives me a lot of joy to see my shoes being worn for years and not dating.

My passion for the past has shaped and moulded me, I have never been influenced by modern fashion. I love the movies of Ernst Lubitsch, George Cukor, Josef von Sternberg and Luis Buñuel; in particular, the close-ups of Catherine Deneuve's feet in *Belle de Jour* wearing a perfect pair of Roger Vivier's Pilgrim pumps. I love the 1950s and the pure classicism of couture, a time when fashion and shoe design was totally linked, and I am inspired by the work of Salvatore Ferragamo, who made glorious shoes out of cork and was incredibly inventive with leftover materials in the 1940s.

For me a fantastic shoe has to have a purity of line, some history behind it, an exuberance of presentation and sometimes I love them just because of who wore them. The designs of my own that I think work the best are the Very Prive, the Love Shoe (because it kept me in business!), the Pigalle, the YSL and my espadrille designs with the low cleavage that were considered bizarre at the time but have now become classics – but I love so many of them!

My long time love of the French showgirl and stage performers means I design a lot of very high heels that lengthen the leg and work best when in movement and combine a lot of elements of fantasy. But people ask all the time, 'How can I walk in these heels?' I answer with the best compliment I remember that came from a woman who lives here in Paris. She said, 'Since I wore your shoes, Christian, I know Paris… I know my street much better. Heels permit me to take the time to look at the architecture of my street. Now I take time to look at things.' High heels give you time to think, to look at your surroundings – a camel has seen more in life than a very quick horse! Women should live to the rhythm of high-heeled shoes!

Christian Louboutin

'00s–'10s   *'20s*   *'30s–'40s*   *'50s*

Introduction

Our obsession with vintage fashion has created a new collectable – the vintage shoe. This untapped market means it has never been a better time to slip your toes into the perfect pair, be it a 1950s stiletto by master craftsman Roger Vivier or a towering 1970s wedge in pastel python skin by Terry de Havilland. Vintage shoes can evoke fashion moments of pure glamour: Marilyn Monroe's scarlet satin rhinestone-studded Ferragamo stilettos are iconic, fused into our collective consciousness because of their starring role in a show-stopping song-and-dance scene in the film *Gentlemen Prefer Blondes* of 1953. The shoe's star power was further reinforced when they were sold at Christie's in New York for $42,000 in 1999.

Even without the magical associations with a famous film star, shoes are still eminently collectable especially when created by the master-craftsmen of shoe design such as André Perugia, Manolo Blahnik, Maud Frizon and Christian Louboutin. Like a classic car, these are high-performance shoes, subtly styled and ergonomically engineered, deluxe and must-have

when first purchased but undervalued in the otherwise buoyant vintage clothing market today.

Is this because shoes still suffer from the associations of practical necessity? Certainly we make contact with the world through our feet – this is why shoes are so significant. Shoes are protective, a necessity of everyday life, allowing us the freedom of mobility we demand in the twenty-first century, and it is significant that when women demand more freedom in culture they wear shoes that are more practical, shoes that make it easier to leave the confines of the home. Shoes then, have meanings and messages that go far beyond mere function and as a result achieve many spectacular forms, from the mordantly practical to the surreally sculptural.

Shoes, like clothes, have the shape-shifting ability to reflect each decade's zeitgeist; Pietro Yanturni's exquisite satin slippers evoke the pampered *grandes horizontales* of the Belle Epoque, a woman of leisure and pleasure who could afford to spend a fortune on personal adornment; the 1920s tango shoe demanded

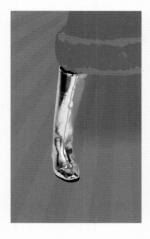

'60s   *'70s*   *'80s*   *'90s–00s*

a different brand of femininity, a ferocious flapper sipping the latest cocktail and rouging her knees for erotic effect. The Charles Jourdan flat calls to mind a string-limbed Twiggy in Swinging '60s London, while many a pair of cone-heeled Manolo Blahniks were sported by power-dressed female executives in the 1980s boardroom.

It is significant that this book opens with the dawn of the twentieth century for this was when mass production changed the shoe market. Shoes were originally produced by hand by the village shoemaker or cobbler (a common occupation in pre-industrial times), and they were relatively expensive items that were supposed to last a lifetime. The mechanization of many aspects of shoe production meant shoes became cheaper and more readily available, demand was stimulated and the market for fashionable shoes rapidly expanded by the first decade of the twentieth century. Women's shoes, in particular, became cheap and cheerful objects of mass consumption with a much shorter lifespan, rejected because they were out of date rather than worn out.

The market has always had room for deluxe brands though, and every decade has its iconic designer shoe. Today shoes have moved from the margins of fashion to the centre. No longer a mere accessory, now they form the focus of a fashionable look, particularly when fashion is at its most minimalist. A sassy pair of Jimmy Choos can lift a jeans and T-shirt combination into fashion's stratosphere and each season there's a frisson of collective anticipation over what delicious designs will be released from the imaginative studios of Manolo Blahnik, Cesare Paciotti and the sublime Christian Louboutin.

This book is designed to be the starting point for any budding collector of vintage shoes and, by charting the history of the twentieth-century shoe in all its major manifestations, gives the visual tools needed to identify significant styles and their designers. For those fascinated by shoes (and who isn't?) this book follows the change from the Louis heels and button boots of the Edwardian era through to the jewel-encrusted collectables of today. Enjoy!

1900-19:
Edwardian Elegance

The Edwardian era was a time of great social change, a period of history in which the conservative values of the Victorian era were being overturned by women who wanted shared ownership of the world. In London and New York, suffragettes were demonstrating for equal rights with men, storming the bastions of patriarchy and vociferously raising questions about the domestic servility of womankind. In the intellectual circles of Vienna, Sigmund Freud was analyzing the relationship between human sexuality and repression, and in Paris, Paul Poiret revolutionized the elite world of haute couture.

For Poiret, mainstream Edwardian fashion made 'over-decorated bundles' of women, so tightly swaddled were they in the frills, furbelows and frou-frou of such an extravagantly decorated look. Couturiers such as Callot-Soeurs, Doucet and Paquin in Paris were tightly corseting women into hourglass shapes with heavy full-length skirts and high-collared boned blouses that made physical activity difficult, and the feminine ideal called for enormous hair-dos padded out for bulk and requiring the ministrations of a maid throughout the day.

In Poiret's theatrical designs, staid Edwardian matrons were radically transformed into sensual, exotic beings, fleshy odalisques awaiting the attentions of their amour in an over-heated Turkish harem or a deeply decadent opium den. His cavalcade of feminine types included Neoclassical nymphs in Empire-line tunics, Oriental femmes fatales in fiery orange and shimmering silver kimono gowns, and bewitching vamps in Indian turbans inspired by Diaghilev's Ballet Russes, which was scandalizing Paris in 1908. Poiret's gowns were shocking; they appeared to have no formal structure, no rigorously laced corsets underneath keeping warm flesh at bay – sensuality was now in vogue. His skirt shapes were also significantly straighter and shorter than ever before, perfect for showing off a shapely ankle rather than just the shy peep of a modest Victorian toe. Shoes came to the forefront of fashion like never before.

The New Woman

As the Edwardian foot became more visible, so tiny feet continued to be prized as erotic symbols of femininity. Many cultures love the small-footed woman; the bound foot of pre-modern China is the most extreme example of this cultural attitude – an attitude that suggests that men's feet are for walking and women's for attracting men. In the nineteenth century, such foot worship was openly displayed in the fashion for Viennese staggerers, boudoir shoes of such extravagant height and tiny length that they blatantly revealed their function was as a fetish object rather than a practicality.

Small feet were also considered a sign of good breeding and gentility, symptomatic of a woman who laboured little and had someone willing to provide for her. Tiny feet were such visible signs of wealth and social status that many women were prepared to suffer in shoes two sizes too small to achieve the right effect. The subsequent pinching created a pain so excruciating that it discouraged walking and perpetuated a degree of domestic dependence.

Change was afoot, though – most notably seen in women's increased appearance on the city streets, whether shopping in the new cathedrals of consumption – the department stores – attending a matinée at the theatre or undertaking philanthropic works among the city's poor. This new social mobility began to be reflected in the design of shoes, with the dainty thin-soled slippers of the Victorian era, which suggested a woman's place was in the home as a demure and decorative object, beginning to be replaced by a sturdier type of day shoe that copied design detail from men's footwear styles such as the Oxford.

Edwardian street shoes for women came in black or tan and had narrow toes, which became broader as the century progressed, arched insteps, Louis heels and leather soles. High-heeled buttoned or laced ankle boots with pliable 'flexura' soles were an everyday fashion staple worn with the new tailor-mades or two-piece suits. This practical look was associated with the 'New Woman', a career-driven creature who rejected the trivial decoration and discomfort of early Edwardian dress, a look that was becoming increasingly anachronistic in the brave new world of the twentieth century.

OVERLEAF Edwardian fashion was decorative, frilly and feminine. A pink pastel gown of 1915 is accessorized with white satin strapped shoes with Louis heels.

RIGHT AND CENTRE The long skirts of the early Edwardian era obscured the feet and emphasized the fashionable S-bend silhouette.

FAR RIGHT A black tiered hobble skirt by Paul Poiret, circa 1915. The couturier's increasingly streamlined skirt designs brought the shoe into view.

Women's increasing input in society was also expressed in their participation in sports. Bicycling had become a craze in the late 1890s and demanded a new form of footwear: the bicycling boot, in black or russet-coloured leather, laced to the knee with a low heel and a ridged sole to prevent the feet from slipping off pedals; and in 1916, the first all-purpose sports shoes were launched onto the market by Keds. They were imaginatively dubbed 'sneakers' by Henry Nelson McKinney, who worked for the advertising agency NW Ayer & Son, because the rubber soles made them perfect for 'sneaking' around. Women also wore canvas shoes or boots with rubber soles for tennis, golf, gymnastics and yachting.

Extravagant shoe design was swept away by the First World War (1914–18), when less flashy styles began to dominate. One of the most striking new silhouettes was the 'war crinoline', which appeared in the designs of Paquin and Jeanne Lanvin. It was a much shorter, fuller skirt that hovered above the ankles and made the slim Poiret style seem inappropriate in a time of crisis. Women's lives continued to undergo significant change and in the new post-war years, low-heeled boots and pumps (or court shoes as they are known in Europe) were the styles predominantly chosen because of their practicality. Pumps were particularly popular as they could be low heeled and low cut with no fastenings, and so could be slipped on and off with ease. A variety of materials were used in shoe construction, including leather mixed with coloured canvas or gabardine to create two-toned shoes called 'spectators'.

Shoe Production and Retail

Up until the 1830s, shoes and boots were sold directly by the craftsmen who made them and footwear remained a handicraft trade. By the mid-nineteenth century, footwear was beginning to be sold through more prestigious outlets, such as drapers, where women gathered to see the new fashions from Paris and to purchase the materials to have their own copies made. The specialist footwear retailer began to emerge in the second half of the nineteenth century: Lilley & Skinner opened in London in 1842 and Florsheim in Chicago in 1904. Florsheim had originally been a wholesaler of shoes, making 150 pairs per day in 1892, which were then sold on to retailers across America who branded them with their own store's name. In 1900, Florsheim mechanized their production by opening a factory that produced shoes under their own brand name, which were then sold through a chain of the company's own specialist footwear stores across North America. They were also the first shoe firm to advertise in national magazines.

America led the way in shoe manufacture with new technology taking over from hand craftsmanship: Isaac Singer's lock-stitch sewing machine, invented in 1856, was able to sew leather as well as cloth; and in 1858, Lyman Blake patented the first machine to attach uppers to soles. Millions of pairs of American shoes were exported to Europe, effectively ending the dominance of French shoe fashion. The mechanization of the shoe industry led to cheaper shoes that many more women could afford. Increased demand meant that fashionable styles could change more rapidly, and new forms of footwear entered the market.

RIGHT The war crinoline of the First World War was a shorter, more practical skirt for the active woman. Here, in 1917, it is worn with a full pleated jacket, a white fox-fur stole and lace-up Louis heels.

ABOVE A coloured Danish magazine illustration of 1914 depicts a woman of fashion trying on but not buying shoes, all with the popular Louis heel.

RIGHT A range of popular women's styles advertised circa 1910. From top: a buckled Cromwell shoe with a Louis heel, an antelope and patent calfskin shoe with Cuban heel, a promenade court shoe with a Cuban heel, a smart strapped shoe in kidskin and patent leather and a white buckskin tennis shoe with a rubber sole.

Bally

One of the first well-known brands in Europe to mechanize the production of their shoes, the Swiss company was created in 1851 when Carl Franz Bally set up a small footwear business in the basement of his house, employing local shoemakers. He had been inspired by the fashionable French slippers he had seen when on a business trip to Paris and had brought several pairs back for his wife – and for his employees to copy. By the 1860s, he had opened a factory using the techniques of mechanized production that had transformed the American footwear industry, and imported many of the new machines into Switzerland, increasing efficiency and, in turn, expanding his company. By 1916, the factory was producing nearly four million pairs of shoes per year, Switzerland's neutrality making it possible for Bally to continue trading in Europe and America during the Great War. Bally's reputation as a manufacturer of well-made, ergonomically designed shoes made from high-quality materials continues today.

The First Shoe Designers

In an era of mechanized shoe production, one of the ways a shoemaker could set himself apart was to advertise his services as a *bottier*, a purveyor of exquisite handmade, hand-fitted shoes. The bottier created 'footwear couture', a shoe that was destined only for the fashionable, wealthy elite, and aped the methods of the grand couturiers such as Charles Frederick Worth and Lucile, Lady Duff Gordon. In the hands of the skilled bottier, shoes could be made that were impossible for a machine to reproduce, so delicate was the handwork and so opulent the embroidered detail. The bottier was no mere artisan but an artist who refused to pander to the demands of his clients, instead creating one-off pairs of shoes as works of art, each made to measure and directly fitted to the customer's feet. For the first time, the names of shoemakers began to be recorded and appeared as *griffes* (signatures) inside the shoes instead of the normal practice of showing the name of the retailer.

Jean-Louis François Pinet (1817–97)

Pinet's is one of the oldest specialist shoe retailers and his store still remains with its original Art Nouveau shop front on London's exclusive Bond Street. The name Pinet now conjures up a high-end store selling wonderful shoes by the world's best designers, but Pinet was originally a shoe designer himself.

François Pinet was born into a family of French shoemakers in Château-la-Vallière, central France, in 1817, and learnt the craft from his father. Seeking fame and fortune in fashion, he arrived in Paris in 1844 to work as a travelling salesman and to learn about the business practices of shoe manufacture. By 1854, he had patented the Pinet heel, a more refined, lighter version of the hourglass-shaped Louis heel, and in 1855, opened a shoe factory specializing in women's footwear in the rue du Petit Lyon Saint Sauvent. He quickly built up a fashionable clientele, and his hand-painted silk boots in luscious colours embellished with intricate gold embroidery or crafted out of supple, shiny kidskin with delicately open-worked uppers were the perfect accompaniment to the gorgeous gowns designed by Charles Frederick Worth, couturier to the Empress Eugénie of France.

After Pinet's retirement, his son took over the family firm and it entered a period of expansion with shops opening in London and Nice. The name became a truly international brand when Pinet's designs were the first shoes to be pictured in an editorial, appearing in *Vogue* in 1909. Renowned shoemakers clamoured to be sold through Pinet's retail outlets throughout the post-war period, including Christian Dior's favourite shoe designer, Roger Vivier.

Pietro Yanturni (1874–1936)

In 1912, the *New York Times* dubbed Yanturni 'the master bootmaker of the world' and wrote of an eccentric figure who lived on a diet of macaroni and water, concentrating all his energies on creating the world's most beautiful shoes.

Born of Italian parentage in Marchesato, Calabria, in 1874, Yanturni was apprenticed to a bootmaker in Naples at the age of 12 and then worked as a journeyman cobbler in France before setting up his own business in Paris in 1904. For the first few years, he concentrated on making wooden forms that shoes were fitted on during production, which he sold to shoemakers. Eventually, he felt skilled enough to create his own shoes and, after a move to new premises in Place Vendôme, hit upon the idea of erecting a sign that said: 'Yantorny: the most expensive shoes in the world'. The intrigue that this generated made him an instant celebrity and had the knock-on effect of self-selecting only the most wealthy clients who could afford his enormous prices.

In his third-floor studio he set about creating delicate shoes that weighed no more than an ostrich feather and soft kid, button boots to adorn the feet of well-heeled women of fashion. His aim was to rid the world of the mundane 'foot boxes' that most women wore, and in their place create works of art inspired by sources as diverse as Elizabeth I, medieval *poulaines* and ancient Tibetan sandals.

PINET FEATURES:
+ The Pinet heel – a refined, more elegant version of the Louis 'wine-glass' heel
+ Extravagant eighteenth-century Rococo revival embroidery
+ 'Barvete & Pinet' or 'F. Pinet' stamped under the instep

YANTURNI FEATURES:
+ Rare antique materials such as lace and velvet
+ Sumptuous embroidery
+ The finest diamond-studded buckles
+ Long, narrow toes and extended tongues

On entering his studio, prospective customers would be entranced by a glass showcase in which were displayed a pair of stunning feathered shoes covered with the tiny quills of 500 Japanese hummingbirds – shoes that had taken six months of intense work to produce. As Yanturni refused to work for any but the most exceptional women with the most beautiful feet, his client list numbered only 20, including the Princess of Greece, who had to pay $3,000 dollars in advance for the privilege of being on his client list – a king's ransom in the early twentieth century. Many had to wait for up to three years to receive a pair of Yanturni shoes.

To achieve the hand-crafted couture fit that was his forte, Yanturni made his customers walk endlessly up and down his studio so that he could study their bare feet in detail. Then, either a plaster cast of each foot was made, on which he moulded his materials, or he would carve a personalized last from a block of mahogany. Yanturni then made up to ten trial pairs of shoes or boots to achieve the exact couture fit he demanded, all destroyed until both he and the client were satisfied. Special stockings were also woven in colours to match each pair of shoes, and were gossamer thin to ensure a perfect fit of foot and shoe.

Yanturni's trademark was the use of rare antique materials, such as eighteenth-century Valenciennes lace or crimson medieval velvet, sourced from the antique dealers and *marches aux puces* (flea markets) of the Portes des Clignancourts. Shoes could be embroidered in gold threadwork or adorned with glittering diamond buckles and were worn by leaders of pre-war fashion, such as Rita de Acosta Lydig, a young divorcee who had received one the largest divorce settlements of the twentieth century from multi-millionaire William Earl Douglas Stokes. She became a famous spendthrift, surrounding herself with fabulous luxury, her pale porcelain skin offset by coal-black hair and an eighteenth-century tricorne hat. Despite (or perhaps because of) never really having to walk anywhere, Lydig had over 300 pairs of Yanturni shoes made from vintage velvet and lace with long toes like twelfth-century poulaines, or broad and square in a mock-Tudor style. Her boudoir slippers in gold brocade or silver silk tissue kept their shape by being stored on shoe trees made from the wood of antique violins, and were kept in custom-made trunks of the finest Russian leather lined with cream panne velvet, one of which now resides in the Metropolitan Museum in New York.

TOP LEFT Nancy Lancaster, socialite and interior designer of Colefax and Fowler fame, commissioned these Genoese red velvet shoes from Yanturni in the early 1920s.

ABOVE LEFT A pair of black silk satin Yanturni shoes, circa 1900–10, with his trademark extended tongues fastened with a rectangular button on the cross strap.

Shoe Etiquette

For women of more modest means, the proliferation of new styles meant different shoes could be worn in a myriad of social situations, and wearing a pair of chic shoes became a new way of expressing one's personal identity. The working woman may have worn one pair of boots all week and then a daintier shoe to church. The wealthier woman, however, could be far more extravagant and change her shoes several times a day if she so wished, from the moment she awoke until she slipped between Egyptian cotton sheets at night – there was no such thing as an all-purpose shoe like today. Wearing several changes of shoe expressed a high degree of taste but, perhaps more importantly, conveyed one's economic status to others. A wealthy woman's myriad of different shoes could include:

Bedroom slippers with thin soles decorated with fur, feather and ribbons.

Bathroom slippers in Moroccan leather or sealskin. They were low heeled and loose fitting because it was believed that feet could become swollen from the hot water used when bathing and therefore they required loose-fitting slippers in which to recover.

Morning boots in Russian leather or antelope skin, front laced with a strong sole.

Indoor luncheon shoes in black velvet or silk with Louis heels.

Afternoon shoes with Louis heels and uppers in kid or antelope.

Racecourse boots in antelope skin, buttoned in grey, dark brown or white, with polished toecaps and a light wooden heel.

Afternoon tea or boudoir slippers, designed to harmonize with the tea gown, in embroidered satin with pointed toes.

Evening shoes, cut low in a décolleté style with a 5- to 6-cm (2- to 2.5-inch) Louis heel in black satin or gold, and silver cloth embroidered with metal wirework.

ABOVE Two fashionable female spectators at the Longchamps races in 1914, dressed in furs and wearing decorative afternoon shoes.

OPPOSITE A daringly short hemline of 1900 displays a pair of black leather day shoes with etched steel buckles.

Signature Shoe Styles

The most significant shoe style of the Edwardian period was the Louis or French heel, which had an hourglass outline that went in at the waist and flared out at the bottom. This combination of graceful shape and sturdy construction meant that the heel was both easy to walk in and elegant to the eye. The high Louis heel also helped to visually reduce the size of the foot by foreshortening it, especially from the front, so that a more comfortable and realistic size of shoe could be worn by women.

The Louis heel was originally invented by Nicholas Lestage in 1660 and popularized by Louis XV (1715–74) at the court of Versailles at a time when heels did not have the feminine connotations they have today. High heels had been in existence since the late sixteenth century and were worn for horse riding as they kept the foot securely in the stirrups, particularly when riding over rough terrain. In the French court of Louis XV, they became

associated with a leisured, pampered existence, a spectacular fashion that literally raised the king above the hoi polloi.

By the early twentieth century, the high heel was both wholly feminine and increasingly erotic as it became more visible beneath women's skirts, with their raised hemlines. Women's heels almost acted as a signpost to the erotic delights above, and the Louis heel had all the seductive connotations of the eighteenth century, conjuring up visions of Madame de Pompadour in her Versailles boudoir. When the Louis heel was combined with a huge gilt, cut steel or marcasite buckle on the front, which acted as a frame for the foot, the shoe looked even more revivalist. Together with the use of decorative brocades and heavy embroidery, this type of footwear gave the impression of a wealthy lifestyle that fell increasingly out of favour during the rigours of the Great War.

OPPOSITE The celebrated actress Miss Fay Evelyn wearing an avant-garde combination of tartan spiral puttees with Louis-heeled shoes in New York, circa 1919. Puttees were originally worn during the Great War by soldiers to protect their lower legs from the mud of the trenches.

LEFT A woman's red leather shoe by Hook Knowles and Co, circa 1900. This low-heeled shoe is laced with a broad red silk ribbon.

BELOW A selection of shoes from the Peter Robinson department store on London's Oxford Street, circa 1904. From top: a beaded strapped evening shoe, a lady's laced and buttoned golf boot and a patent leather steel-buckled shoe with Louis heel.

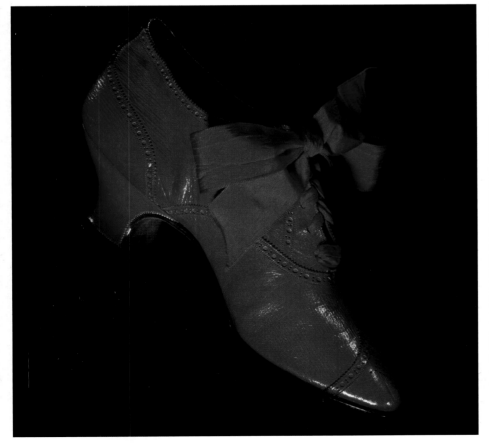

PETER ROBINSON'S
OXFORD STREET.

FINE EXAMPLE OF BEADED SHOES, open cut at sides and on vamp, making a very attractive shoe.

No. 824

Price
21/6

LADIES' GOLF BOOTS, black and brown leathers, laced to ankle, and buttoned gaiter tops. Excellent wear.

No. 262

Price
25/6

BEAUTIFULLY MODELLED EVENING SHOE, patent leather or glace kid, Louis XV. heels, and handsome steel slide.

No. 334

Price
21/6

Letter orders despatched immediately.
PETER ROBINSON Ltd.
OXFORD STREET.

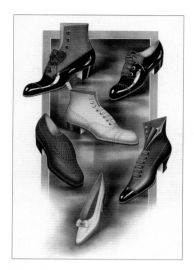

Button Boots

In this period, boots or *bottines* were the accepted everyday footwear for both men and women. Boots are one of the most archaic forms of footwear, depicted in prehistoric cave painting and unearthed from pharaohs' tombs. Fundamentally practical, throughout history boots were long associated with horse riding and the military but, when worn by women, were more delicate, encasing a tiny foot and laced or buttoned to the ankles.

In the Edwardian period, women wore both front-laced and button boots. Button boots were the tightest fitting and most fiddly to get on as the buttons had to be closed with a button hook, a difficult task compellingly described by writer Eileen Elias in 1910:

The buttonholes were so hard and slit-like that they hurt your fingers, and you didn't always have a button hook. Even if you had, it invariably hooked the wrong button into the hole. I would sit wrestling with my button boots and choking back tears. As often as not I would be forced to walk out into the road with the buttons half undone, and pretend not to notice the grins and glances.

The close fit of the correctly buttoned boot made the foot and ankle appear slim, operating almost like a corset for the foot, but there was no gain without pain. For, once on, the tight boot had to stay on all day and no adjustment was possible, which caused innumerable aches and pains. Front-laced boots were a more practical alternative as they could be adjusted relatively easily when on the foot and were preferred by the more active woman as a result. The most functional had broad toes and low heels, a rather masculine look that was exacerbated when many were made using male lasts.

Red boots were something of a fad in the late Victorian and early Edwardian era, lavishly inlaid with gold kid by Pinet or decorated with embroidery or metal threadwork. They were considered the most openly alluring of footwear types, perhaps because of their high status origins. Red was traditionally the colour of cardinals' robes and aristocratic outfits as it was the most expensive dye to produce, derived from madder and the crushed shells of cochineal beetles.

By the nineteenth century, the fashion for the red shoe, usually of expensive Moroccan leather, began to infiltrate women's footwear, and in 1868, the introduction of synthetic or aniline red dyes meant that red shoes were considerably cheaper than they had ever been in the past. The visual impact they made and their rather saucy colour made them popular among the can-can dancers of the Moulin Rouge and the *grandes horizontales* (courtesans) of the Belle Epoque.

La Belle Otero was one of the most internationally renowned of this demi-monde, with a scandalous lifestyle and provocative image that shocked Europe

TOP LEFT A catalogue of elegant buttoned and laced boots and shoes from the popular *Penrose Annual* of 1912.

ABOVE Pearl White was one of the silent film era's most successful stars after starring in the serial *The Perils of Pauline* (1914). Here she wears a costume from *The Fatal Ring* (1917) that includes long-toed laced silk boots.

FLOWERS ON HER STOCKINGS AND GEMS NEAR HER TOES!

CORONATION HOSE WITH PAINTED DECORATION AND CORONATION SHOES WITH PAINTED TOES.

ABOVE Hand-painted stockings and gem-encrusted and embroidered shoes were all the rage in Britain during the Coronation year of King George V, in 1911.

BELOW A pair of white satin strapped shoes from the first decade of the twentieth century, intricately beaded and fastened with pearls.

until she died unrepentant at the age of 97. She was known for a lascivious fandango that she performed in the early 1900s on the tables at the Parisian restaurant Maxim's, where she flashed her high front-laced boots of silver or red kidskin – it a wild dance, so erotic that one male observer confessed his 'thighs were blushing'.

Boudoir Slippers

The Edwardian boudoir was a woman's space in which she swapped her formal clothes for a relaxed tea gown and kicked off her Louis heels in favour of a pair of pretty boudoir slippers. Boudoir slippers were a form of casual shoe that had been in existence since the eighteenth century, when the boudoir began to be added to wealthy homes and was regarded as a place where women gathered to gossip or get over grievances – boudoir comes from the French 'bouder' meaning 'to sulk'. Boudoirs were informal and feminine, decorated in a French Rococo revival style, and their owners had clothing to match. Tea gowns in frothy lace with satin sashes delineating the waist were popular, worn with either matching satin slippers, which were backless and flat, or mules with a Louis heel and a thin leather sole.

Pink was the most popular colour, and the vamp (upper part) of the boudoir slipper was usually of satin or velvet and covered in Rococo embroidery, a style that had been revived by Michonet, the master embroiderer at the House of Worth, the design house of Charles Frederick Worth. One of the most popular forms was ribbon embroidery, a three-dimensional style that used a combination of ribbon and silk floss with traditional embroidery stitches to give a sumptuous padded effect. Other popular decorative devices included inserts of gold lace or black jet beading, which, when combined with pink, cream or red, made a dramatic contrast. These delicate forms of footwear were tied at the ankle with satin ribbons or a ribbon across the instep. Many women crafted their own boudoir slippers to match their favourite gowns, and women's magazines contained patterns that meant the latest fashions could be produced at home. The uppers were embroidered and then taken to the local cobbler to have soles attached.

The most successful purveyor of boudoir slippers in the early twentieth century was the American firm Daniel Green. Green himself was a travelling shoe salesman for the Wallace Elliott Company in New York, and when visiting a felt mill he noticed that many of the workers were wearing flat slippers made entirely of pieces of discarded felt to shield their feet from the cold of the factory floor. He persuaded the mill owner to manufacture felt slippers to sell to the shoe trade with himself as sole agent and, in 1885, when pretty colours, white felt soles and heels were added for the boudoir, he sold 75,000 pairs. One hundred million pairs of shoes later, the firm is still in operation and Green's original Edwardian slippers are avidly collected by vintage footwear enthusiasts.

Dancing Shoes

In 1914, the *New York Times* wrote: 'Anyone can dance an old-fashioned waltz in a shoe that sags at the heel, pinches through the arch and binds through the instep. But nobody can dance one of the modern dances in an uncomfortable shoe.' One of the modern dances the newspaper was referring to was the tango, a scandalous dance craze that had been imported from Argentina in the early twentieth century. The dance was openly erotic, sensuous and flamboyant and was an immediate success, especially when taught by young, brilliantined gauchos imported from Rio de Janeiro – although it had to be enormously modified to be acceptable to an Edwardian audience. In 1913 in London, 'tango teas' came into fashion in hotels and restaurants that had enough floor space for dancing, and exhibition dancers such as Irene and Vernon Castle showed a willing audience the correct steps and attitude. Tango shoes had a low Louis heel, which was practical for dancing, and were laced up the ankle with a criss-crossed ribbon, some with a multi-strap or barrette front.

The Bare·Legged American Babes.

MARY AND DOUGLAS OF THE NEW OXFORD PANTO : THE DOLLY SISTERS.

The Dolly Sisters are dubbed Mary and Douglas in their panto parts as the Babes in the Wood, at the New Oxford; and Charlie and the Kid are sent to murder them—a task which is badly bungled. Rosie Dolly is Mary; Jenny Dolly plays Douglas. It may seem strange to have American-born Babes—with bare legs, too, for one Dolly at least gives stockings "a miss"—but the fascinations of Rosie and Jenny are as powerful in pantomime as in revue. Our photographs show the Dollys after they have grown up in a night, by fairy magic.

Photographs by Foulsham and Banfield, Ltd.

LEFT Irene and Vernon Castle popularized the tango for a mainstream American audience. Irene (1893–1969) was one of the first women to bob her hair and wear Louis-heeled tango shoes.

ABOVE The Dolly Sisters, twins Rose and Jenny Deutsch, were Hungarian émigrés who became a popular vaudeville act in the 1910s and 1920s. Here Jenny reveals bare legs and buckles, Rose a pair of laced-up tango shoes.

OPPOSITE A pair of black leather Louis heels from 1916, with cut-out details across the vamp and accessorized with rather racy garters at the knees with feather rosettes (just seen).

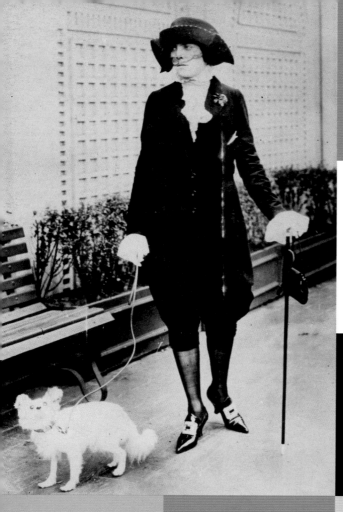

◄ **Historical references**
Edwardian shoes make many references to a romantic vision of the eighteenth century. Here, a woman in a dashing tricorne hat wears a pair of Cromwell-style buckled day shoes with Louis heels. The fashion for buckles dominated eighteenth-century footwear and this decorative device was successfully revived in the early twentieth century.

Key looks of the decade

1900-19

◄ **The Louis heel**
The Louis heel was the most popular pre-war heel shape, seen here on a red leather shoe and a bright mauve suede buckled shoe, both circa 1900. Edwardian Louis heels were a sturdier and more practical version of their eighteenth-century counterpart and their wine-glass shape could be seen on every city street.

▲ **Extended toes and lengthened vamps**
Both male and female shoes had a similar silhouette, which included a long slim toe on an extended vamp. A woman's crocodile day shoe is seen next to a man's black leather boot. Women expected a certain degree of discomfort in order to achieve the ladylike dainty foot.

▸ Balmoral boots

A pair of black leather and green suede Balmoral boots by Crockett and Jones of Northampton, circa 1900–19. They were named after Balmoral Castle, Scotland, after Queen Victoria had it rebuilt and refurbished for her personal use in the 1850s. As skirts became shorter, the medium-height Balmoral boot became taller and front lacing replaced buttons.

Lace-up boots

Lacing as a means of fastening boots became a fashionable alternative to buttons because of their ability to act like close fitting 'corsets for the feet' and they could be adjusted throughout the day.

◂ Evening shoes

Dancing became more energetic in the 1910s and required shoes that could be affixed more securely to the feet. The low-heeled bar-strap shoe fitted the bill, here in glamorous gold leather.

◂ Button boots

Boots with buttoned gaiters were worn for many outdoor and sporting activities such as cycling, golfing and walking, usually with a skirt that rose up to 15 cm (6 inches) off the ground. The men's boots (top) are in patent leather with a fawn cloth gaiter, circa 1900, while the women's are in grey suede and date from 1910.

1920s:
The Modernist Shoe

Modernism changed the look of the shoe in the 1920s, as Cubist aesthetics, Bauhaus austerity and American streamlining entered the vocabulary of the designer in the form of Art Deco. This style reached its apotheosis at the Exposition des Arts Décoratifs, held in Paris in 1924, where the exhibits revealed the hallmarks of this innovative style: a combination of clear lines and geometric shapes rendered out of the most deluxe of materials.

Shoes followed suit and as their lines became increasingly simple, so the materials used to make the uppers became more exotic. Colours were bold and bright and surface decoration graphic – Chinese, Cubist or Egyptian-inspired after the discovery of Tutankhamen's tomb in 1922. Rows of buttons and intricate laces, so popular at the beginning of the century, were rejected in favour of styles that had more visual clarity, such as single side buttons and T-bar shapes. Cuban heels took over from the hourglass Louis heel and, when affixed to evening shoes, were extravagantly decorated with rhinestones, mock tortoiseshell or cloisonné enamel.

The uncluttered silhouettes of Paul Poiret influenced a new generation of couturiers including Coco Chanel and Madeleine Vionnet, who presented a *sportif* silhouette that reflected the prevailing zeitgeist of youth and modernity and revealed, as Chanel described, 'the death of luxury'. Luxury was still there, however, albeit in a more understated form of 'deluxe poverty'. Simple cloche hats were worn over short, chic bobbed haircuts, and womanly hips and breasts were out of fashion. In their place came a more elegantly androgynous, tubular look, with simple skirts hovering around the knee, which gave focus to the entire shoe rather than just the toe as in previous years. Little black cocktail dresses were matched with little black shoes in satin or patent leather. The more visible shoe made a woman's fashion savvy more obvious – now it was clear whether she was keeping abreast of shoe trends or not.

The painted faces and short hemlines of the flappers presented a more overt sexuality when sashaying down the city streets and caused alarm among more traditional members of the public, who suspected, quite rightly, that fashionable femininity was in transition. Women claimed the right to roam and by so doing were breaking societal and sometimes sartorial codes. By appearing on their own, without male chaperones on the city streets, wearing obvious make-up and brazenly smoking Russian cigarettes from ivory holders, they were playing with the codes of femininity by aping the modes and manners of the vamp.

Dance Shoes and Decoration

Edwardian society had retained vestiges of the aristocratic but the 1920s were different; class structure was beginning to break down and many more members of the community shared an increased prosperity and better living conditions. More money was being spent on fashion and more money was being spent on fun. The two came together in the dance revolution that had begun with the Argentinean tango and was expressed in an even wilder way with the dance innovations of the 1920s.

The rise of ragtime and jazz – syncopated, rhythmic musical forms originating from black America – brought about a new freedom in dancing and created energetic styles such as the Bunny Hug, where couples pressed their bodies tightly together, and the fast-paced Turkey Trot, a spirited reaction against the inhibited and formal movements of the traditional waltz. In 1919, one vicar was even moved to protest, 'If these up-to-date dances, described as the "latest craze" are within a hundred miles of all I hear about them, I should say that the morals of a pig-sty would be respectable in comparison.'

The Charleston was no better, introduced to the American public as part of the Ziegfeld Follies show *Runnin' Wild* in 1923, and reaching Europe by 1925. Its celebrated side-kicks and exaggerated play with the knees required a much sturdier shoe for women to participate with any degree of athleticism. Shoes became more securely fitted to the feet, with low Cuban heels and closed toes, and beaded decoration and metallic threadwork that glittered in the lights of a smoky speakeasy. When matched with a beaded and fringed dance dress, women shimmered spectacularly in contrast to their black-suited partners. If more glitz was needed, an array of shoe clips were available in the form of birds, Egyptian scarabs and butterflies, which could be added to little black day shoes to create instant party feet. Cubist patterns, hand-painted Chinoiserie and daring colour combinations entered the market – a cacophony of gold and red kidskin, sky-blue and emerald-green satin, or more subtle black velvet with steel beadwork. More prosaically, improved manufacturing processes meant that significantly cheaper shoes were available, so many were chosen simply because of their looks rather than their more practical function.

OVERLEAF In the 1920s the silhouette became more streamlined with shorter hair and skirts and graphic shoe shapes. A model of 1925 wears a little black dress trimmed with lace frills and pointed toed shoes with oversized square buckles.

ABOVE A selection of evening pumps. From top, a kidskin evening pump with a scalloped trim of pearlized lizard by Vida Moore; an embroidered crepe-de-chine strapped shoe with scalloped edges also by Moore; and a silver lamé high-heeled pump with a jewelled buckle on a silver kidskin strap from Delman.

RIGHT The latest white fur fashion and cloche hat is teamed with burnished satin evening shoes with bar straps, circa 1926. The new flapper style emphasized a long leg and shapely ankle, rather than the Edwardian hourglass silhouette.

OPPOSITE TOP A pair of black satin button-bar shoes is accompanied by an anklet made from shiny black Whitby jet, circa 1920. The ankle and lower leg, no longer hidden away under long sweeping skirts, become a focal point.

OPPOSITE CENTRE From top, a pale eau-de-nil velvet shoe with a green diamanté fastening from Edward Rayne, 1928; a brown satin evening shoe by Stead and Simpson, decorated with a golden hand-painted phoenix from 1922; and a 1925 golden kidskin T-bar dancing shoe by A Rambaldi, covered in hand-painted flowers.

OPPOSITE BOTTOM Both shoes and stockings became more decorative in the mid 1920s. Here evening shoes with a crossed bar strap, are teamed with stockings embellished with a faux gem ankle bracelet.

DECORATIVE ELEMENTS:

+ Shoe clips, especially in insect and butterfly shapes, that could be added to shoes for an instant party feel
+ Geometric Cubist patterns
+ Hand-painted chinoiserie details
+ Daring colour combinations such as silver and tango orange
+ Metallic threadwork and beadwork
+ Egyptian and Native American motifs
+ Heels made of Bakelite, Wedgwood and Jasperware, and decorated with rhinestones and beading

ABOVE A brocade shoe of 1925 has the added glamour of a pearl-studded silver buckle.

ABOVE RIGHT A bobbed flapper shows off a selection of shoe jewellery, circa 1928. Clips were an easy and cheap way to completely change the look of a simple evening shoe and could be used to complement any shade of evening gown.

RIGHT A pair of buttercup yellow satin pearl-button bar shoes with a darker toned crepe-de-chine and turquoise rosette detail, circa 1920–25.

OPPOSITE A minimalist yet deluxe Art Deco interior, all simple lines and glamorous fashion. A model sports a cocktail dress with velvet skirt and elegant high-heeled evening pumps with square rhinestone-studded shoe clips, circa 1928..

A key change in the 1920s was the disappearance of the boot, so beloved of the Edwardian woman. The newly shortened skirt created an unsightly gap between the top of the boot and the hem of the skirt, a gap that yawned wider and wider as the decade progressed. Eventually, boots were ditched in favour of short-toed bar shoes with high wooden heels and sheer stockings, which made the legs (and an artfully rouged pair of knees) look enticingly erotic. Rubber galoshes or overshoes were worn during inclement weather, which removed the necessity for boots, another reason for their demise. Many young women refused to fasten the buckles that secured the galosh about the ankle, leaving it flapping rather wetly against the calf. This relaxed informal look, some believe, gave rise to the word 'flapper' to describe the new, seemingly strident young woman of the 1920s.

Such an abrupt change in footwear etiquette shocked the older generation, who had very strict ideas about what should be worn, where, and when. As early as 1916, the *Shoe and Leather Lexicon*, an American trade magazine, wrote that 'Women have shown a tendency in late years to wear on the street shoes suitable only for indoor use… desiring to drag boudoir suggestiveness through the streets.' In the 1920s, the standards of usage began to seriously slip quite simply because with so many styles to choose from, young women were determined to wear whatever they pleased. A few rules still applied, however, although they were less rigorously implemented than in the previous decade:

Day shoes covered more of the foot than those designated as eveningwear, which had lower-cut vamps (upper parts).

Stacked leather heels were for practical daywear; the dressier Louis heel was for night. Evening shoes had higher and more thinly tapered heels.

Toe caps signified a day shoe; plain toes were for evening.

Sport shoes had brogueing or perforation along the seams, following the rules of traditional male sports footwear.

Suede and leather in brown or black were supposed to be for daywear, and fabric for night only, although many women ignored this distinction.

LEFT A line of chorus girls from *The Girl from Cooks* show, 1927, display T-bar, split-bar and strappy cut-out dancing shoes.

TOP A winter outfit of fur-trimmed coat and boots with spats, circa 1925. Boots had become items of functional footwear rather than being worn for everyday as in the preceeding decades. They only appeared when needed in inclement weather.

ABOVE The Hollywood actress Bessie Love, circa 1928, gets ready for the rain. Galoshes were worn unfastened to give a more casual girl-about-town look. Their untidy appearance gave rise to the epithet 'flapper'.

ABOVE Ladies' solo
Charleston champion Miss
Hardie, who danced for a
record seven hours in 1925,
wears low sturdy heels and
a bar strap to keep her
shoes secure during her
energetic dance routine.

RIGHT A Liberty's of London
outfit from 1928, worn with a
simple leather bar shoe,
a 1920s fashion favourite.
The Mary Jane was a
version of this standard item
of footwear with a rounder
toe and shorter heel.

The Mary Jane and Signature Shoes

The Mary Jane was a broad, closed-toed shoe with a flat single strap that fastened across the instep, with a button to the side and a low heel. It has a long history as a child's shoe and can be seen in Tudor paintings of the sixteenth century. This shoe had important symbolic associations because it traditionally signalled a child's transition from baby to toddler, as it was worn when a child took his or her first tentative steps. The shoe thus symbolized a significant rite of passage.

By the early twentieth century, this eminently practical style of footwear was yet to be given a gender and remained a unisex children's shoe. It was worn by such resonant childhood fictional characters as Alice in Wonderland, and Christopher Robin in the well-known illustrations by EH Shepherd for AA Milne's *Winnie the Pooh*. However, events conspired to make this shoe feminine, an item fit only for a woman's wardrobe, where it remains to this day.

In 1902, a cartoon strip called 'Buster Brown' appeared in the *New York Herald* newspaper, created by graphic artist Richard F Outcault and featuring a group of mischievous children, which included the eponymous Buster Brown, his dog, Tige, and his sister, Mary Jane. The popularity of the cartoon was such that in 1904, Outcault visited the St Louis World's Fair with the express intention of cashing in on his creations. He allowed 200 manufacturers licences to use his characters as brand names, one of which was the Brown Shoe Company, which had been set up with the life savings of one George Warren Brown in 1878.

Buster Brown became the brand that built the shoe empire that the Brown Shoe Company is today, with its annual turnover of over $2 billion. The company's success is in part due to this licensing deal, which was used to create a pioneering marketing campaign. From 1904 onwards, a roadshow travelled across America visiting department stores and shoe shops, featuring actors dressed as characters from the cartoon strip. Thousands of clamouring kids persuaded their mothers to buy into the brand name, in an early example of cartoon merchandizing that pre-dated Walt Disney.

Mary Jane, Buster Brown's sister, was immortalized when her name was applied to single-strap children's shoes in 1909, and the shoes gradually transformed into items of female dress, eventually totally disappearing from the male wardrobe. Their sugary sweet feminine associations were also fused on celluloid when adopted by the world's most popular (and saccharine) child star, Shirley Temple. She first tap danced her way across the silver screen in the shoes in 1922's *Baby Burlesk*, and they continued to be her only form of footwear throughout her reign as the world's most popular child star. With her carefully coiffed ringlets, fixed grin and party dresses puffed out with starched petticoats, Shirley Temple gave Mary Jane shoes an image of such exaggerated girliness that it was only really shaken off by the post-modernist play of ravaged rock star Courtney Love and her ironic Mary Jane wearing in the 1990s.

When flappers adopted the Mary Jane shoe in the 1920s, they were deliberately choosing a shoe style that evoked youthfulness – the aesthetic that was the prime force behind fashionable trends, in particular the slim, streamlined, almost schoolgirl silhouette with flattened breasts and skirts that skimmed the hips. Fashions of the 1920s deliberately rejected any hint of the matron, and the Mary Jane shoe, the most childish of shoe shapes, was a perfect foil for this fashion.

Over the decade, though, Mary Janes subtly changed and towards the end of the 1920s, their heels became higher and more tapered, their plain cloth or leather uppers more deluxe, and the look of innocence subverted with the use of sensuous satins, heavy brocades and hand-painted silks. The little girl appeared to be growing up.

BELOW Evening shoes of 1925. Both day and evening styles became increasingly decorative and combined multicoloured leather with fabrics such as brocade, satin and silk. Heels were higher and more tapered.

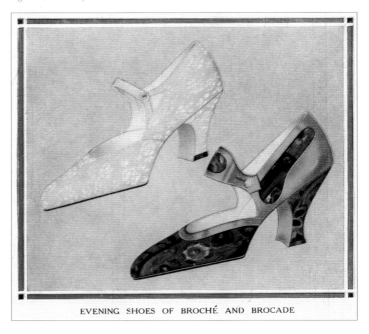

EVENING SHOES OF BROCHÉ AND BROCADE

The Strapped Shoe

The most innovative design detail in 1920s shoes was the use of elaborate strapwork. This was a fashion element that started out with shoes that incorporated one, or occasionally two, horizontal straps with contrasting coloured stitching fastened with a simple button at the side. By 1922, the T-strap was introduced, a strap that ran vertically down the front of the shoe with another strap across to form a 'T' shape, again fastened at the side with a button. The new T-strap was often delineated in contrasting colours so as to stand out against the rest of the shoe. It was an instant success, as it streamlined a woman's foot while saucily exposing it, evoking a frisson of fashionable bondage while simultaneously creating an elegantly modernist shape that was the height of fashion.

OPPOSITE A fashion model wears a sleeveless loose-fitting dress with a monochromatic striped and fringed skirt, double-strap Mary Jane shoes and a headband, circa 1925.

ABOVE RIGHT Edward Steichen photographed a model's feet in white T-bar shoes with a contrasting black trim for this evocative beach scene of 1925.

RIGHT American actress Eleanor Boardman is seen here wearing late 1920s cutaway shoes with front-fastening clasps.

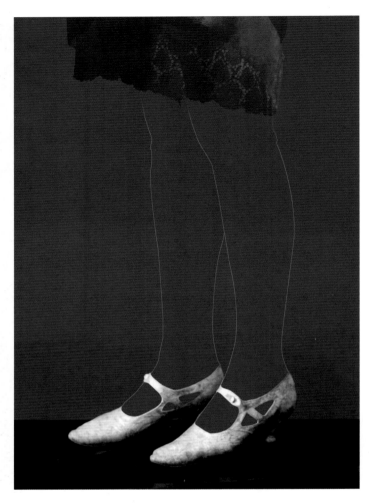

The use of strapwork in shoe design continued, becoming almost fetishist in its application by the middle of the decade. In 1923, for instance, the back of the shoe was extended up the ankle to form an ankle strap that was then fixed to a T-bar in the front. Faux strapwork was also popular, taking the form of intricate leather cut-outs that covered the sides and front of shoes in a finely wrought filigree of leather, which was edged in gold, silver and contrasting coloured skin on the most expensive shoes. Fixed buckles began to take over from buttons as fastening devices and continued to be popular into the 1930s, either in simple steel or more elaborate Art Deco designs studded with sparkling marcasite.

ABOVE These decoratively cutaway bar shoes with Louis heels are from the early 1920s.

RIGHT Illustrations of high-heeled court shoes with elongated toes, shown in the *Gazette du Bon Ton* magazine of 1924. From top: a multiple loop shoe, a T-bar, a double-loop. and a style with a strap secured with a leaf-shaped bar.

LEFT Silver metallic
T-bar shoes with a
Louis heel worn with
patterned stockings
and a metal garter, fresh
from 1920s Paris.

The Russian Boot

The solid leg boot with no fastenings in an easy pull-on, pull-off style had first appeared for women in 1915, but this experimental style failed to catch on possibly because skirts were just too long for the boot to be practical. It was re-introduced with more success as the Russian boot in 1921.

The 1920s Russian boot was knee high, wide topped and flat, based on the traditional Russian *valenki*, a boot that had been developed to cope with the severe winters of Siberia. The valenki was a rustic boot, similar in shape to a Wellington or an Australian Ugg boot today, and was made out of thick felt with no seams. Its function, practicality and ease of removal had made it a key part of the Russian soldier's winter kit by the nineteenth century.

Young flappers adopted the silhouette of the *valenki* when it was re-created as a fashion rather than folk item, rendered in leather and given a low Louis or Cuban heel in 1921. In 1927, the style was endorsed by Hollywood star Gloria Swanson when she advertised a pair of Russian boots for Sears, Roebuck and Company – quite a brave step to take, as by then Russian boots had developed a reputation as the chosen form of footwear for girls who flirted with the underworld.

In 1922, a young woman in Chicago had been photographed in a speakeasy mischievously concealing a flask of illegal liquor down the side of one boot – a perfect illustration of the practice of 'bootlegging', a term that dates back to the nineteenth century. Bootleggers were those who hid whiskey in their boot tops when going to trade with Native Americans, and it became a byword for criminals involved in the illegal transportation of alcohol across state lines. By 1920, bootlegging had become a part of general vocabulary when the National Prohibition Act was passed banning the export, import, transportation, selling and manufacture of alcohol in an attempt to reduce crime and promote healthy and moral lifestyles.

Drinking went underground as illegal speakeasies and saloon bars flourished in most major American cities and every town had its own illegal still, making cheap moonshine for those who wished to imbibe. The Russian boot evoked the image of a woman who walked on the wild side, who was prepared to risk her reputation in order to have a good time – and it was a much sexier alternative to rubber galoshes. By 1930, however, the style had peaked and died, destined to lie dormant until the 1960s.

The Oxford

Sometimes referred to as the Balmoral in the United Kingdom, the Oxford is a classic piece of male footwear design that laces up in the front, usually through three pairs of eyelets; it has a tongue to protect the foot from the pressure of the fastenings, curved side seams and a low-stacked leather heel. By the early twentieth century, this practical and comfortable style had been adopted by women and it became the most favoured style of street shoe in the 1920s, when a 5-cm (2-inch) heel was added. The heels became higher and more finely tapered by the middle years of the decade, as the shoe moved from being a staple of the male wardrobe into a female form of fashion.

There were many nuances in women's Oxford shoe design, all appropriated from traditional male footwear styles. The laces were enclosed, wingtips (so-called because the shape resembled the spread wings of a bird) or brogueing detail were sometimes added as perforated panels of decoration along the sides and across the toes, and a small piece of leather was often stitched over the toe to create a toe cap. Saddle Oxfords had a saddle-shaped section sewn onto the upper quarter of the vamp that was of a contrasting colour to the rest of the shoe.

Sports Oxfords or 'spectator' shoes, so-called because they were supposed to be worn by spectators standing on the sidelines of sporting events, had heels and saddles of a different colour to the rest of the shoe. As many spectator shoes had vamps of white

canvas, the toes and heels were made of leather to protect the parts of the shoe that were liable to scuff. Popular colour combinations were black-and-white patent or brown-and-tan leather, and the more fashion-forward girl about town wore a mix of shiny black patent and brightly coloured reptile skin.

Between 1925 and 1927, the fashion for cut-outs infiltrated the Oxford, appearing next to the eyelets and banishing the tongue, and the toes began to be elongated, so much so that it was difficult to tell whether the style was actually an Oxford or not. This rather mongrel shoe type was given the catch-all term of semi-Oxford.

Mistinguett

Legs, feet and shoes were more overtly displayed in this decade than ever before and the display of a neat pair of pins in beige artificial silk stockings presented what appeared to be a naked leg, creating a new area of erotic interest for men. The most beautiful pair were the property of French showgirl Mistinguett, who was the toast of Paris in the 1920s and was rumoured to have insured her legs for a million dollars. They were displayed to stunning effect during her long-running residency at the Folies Bergère. The climax of the show had Mistinguett – resplendent in an ostrich-feather headdress that weighed 7 kilograms (15 pounds) and a stage outfit with a 25-metre (82-foot) long train – descend a steep staircase in very high heels. Little did the rapt audience know that her eyes were tightly shut to aid concentration and overcome vertigo, because a pair of fake eyes were painted on her closed eyelids in stage make-up.

When off stage, Mistinguett still showed her legs to their best advantage and highlighted them with exaggeratedly high heels, created by the celebrated shoe designer André Perugia. For Mistinguett he fashioned a pair of extravagantly fetishist mules with green suede heels, gold speckled suede vamps in a trompe l'oeil speckled leather effect, to mimic snakeskin, and a vampish ocelot edging – perhaps the most overtly erotic pairs of shoes ever made.

OPPOSITE An illustrative poster of 1913 depicts a seductive Mistinguett in elaborately decorative fantasy footwear.

BELOW The infamous French showgirl and music-hall star Mistinguett with her vast collection of high-heeled shoes. She shows off her celebrated legs.

MISTINGUETT

G.K. Benda

Affiche DÉPOSÉE

PHILIPPE·G·DREYFUS. Editeur. 13. Rue Lafayette. PARIS

André Perugia (1893–1977)

Known for his experimentation with new materials, shapes and textures, André Perugia's shoe designs dominated high-end footwear fashion in the 1920s and remain some of the most innovative and experimental footwear ever created for women. Perugia's most successful work was for Saks Fifth Avenue, who distributed his ready-to-wear Padova brand, the American company I Miller, with whom he had a 50-year association, and Charles Jourdan, for whom he was a technical advisor from 1962 to 1966. Like Pietro Yanturni, Perugia, the son of a cobbler, had a background far removed from the elite world of haute couture, although that is where he eventually made his mark, designing shoes for Jacques Fath, Edward Molyneux and the House of Schiaparelli in the 1930s.

Born in Tuscany, Perugia worked as an apprentice in his father's workshop, which was set up when the family moved to Nice in the early 1900s, and by the age of 16, he had taken over the family business. Nice was a popular seaside location where the rich of Paris gathered to spend languid summers sequestered in the hotels that lined the city's fashionable promenade and to gamble away fortunes in its many casinos. Perugia realized that here was a perfect audience for his wares and persuaded one of the top hotels, the Negresco, to devote a window to his shoe designs.

Not only did he draw the attention of the female patrons, but the window display also caught the eye of Paul Poiret in 1914, who from that moment on took the young Perugia under his wing, inviting him to present his shoes in Poiret's *atelier* in Paris and to meet a wealthier, more fashion-fixated clientele. Perugia's shoes were also used to accessorize several of the

couturier's fashion shows that were being held in Nice during the summer season. However, this potentially lucrative breakthrough in Perugia's career was cut short by the First World War and he was requisitioned to work in an aircraft factory. This seemingly unfortunate turn of events was in fact to have an enormously beneficial impact on his aesthetic. Surrounded by the machinery of the military, Perugia was introduced to engineering techniques that were to transform his ideas about shoe design and lead to the development of a series of prototype aerodynamic heels in steel alloy, which anticipated the stiletto heel of the 1950s. For him, shoe design was about precision; as he put it, 'a pair of shoes must be perfect like an equation, and adjusted to the millimetre like a motor piece.'

André Perugia began to seriously make his name in the 1920s, after opening his own shop on the rue du Faubourg Saint-Honoré in 1921, working with Hollywood film stars Pola Negri and Gloria Swanson, for whom his black lace heels became something of a trademark, and the stage star Josephine Baker, for whom he designed quilted kidskin sandals. He also continued his relationship with Paul Poiret, creating the Arlequinade and Folie shoes, named after two of the House of Poiret's most popular fragrances. In 1924, in homage to the couturier's patronage, Perugia created Le Bal, a whimsical pair of shoes that celebrated Poiret's renowned love of parties (which eventually contributed to his financial ruin). Each shoe was heavily over-embroidered with a pattern of densely placed seed beads that showed, in vignette form, on one shoe a portrait of Poiret and on the other his wife and muse, Denise – and they caused a fashionable furore when she entered a crowded ballroom.

OPPOSITE Footwear legend André Perugia in his shoe factory, circa 1951, among a multitude of handmade wooden lasts. For an average shoe style a total of 600 patterns, one for every vamp and quarter, was made to give a full range of lengths and widths. His first boutique opened in 1921.

BELOW A reassuringly expensive and refined satin sandal-pump by Perugia from 1929, with a looped T-bar.

Every season, Perugia made sure he hit the headlines with some flamboyant experimental design, but these tended to be one-offs. The rest of his time was spent producing chic, wearable shoes that followed the prevailing silhouette, albeit more exquisitely made than most. Thus, his 1920s designs followed the fashion for T-bars and straps with fantastic finishes, such as burnished bronze and gold metal with Art Deco motifs moulded in relief on tapering heels, and intricate Cubist patterns cut out of leather inlay. He became known for using the most remarkable diversity of exotic materials: glossy black horsehair, antelope and alligator, even Peruvian llama. His forte was combining materials such as champagne-coloured satin and metallic brocade or gold leather with velvet dyed exactly the same shade, so as to give a tactile as well as a visual appeal to the shoe. Fastenings were given the same detailed attention: buckles were exquisitely carved and enamelled and buttons took on the shape of diminutive gilded rosebuds.

What differentiated Perugia from earlier footwear designers such as Yanturni or Pinet was that, as a result of his engineering background, he was the first to really understand the ergonomics of shoe design. Like those before him, he always took an impression of the client's foot in plaster of Paris and made detailed measurements, but for him the most fascinating part of shoe design was working out the relationship between the shoe and the heel and how weight was distributed through the body and onto the feet. Suitability, function and the relationship of the shape of the shoe to the correct balance of the heel were, for him, more important than any fashionable design. To this end, he literally took the shoe apart

and re-assembled it, achieving designs by the 1950s that totally transformed the look of women's shoes.

Throughout his career, Perugia kept developing totally new methods of manufacture and construction, applying for over 40 patents for his innovative designs such as the corkscrew heel of 1952. Shoes became sculpture in his magical hands; the 'Ode to Industry' shoe of 1950, for instance, was more of an art object than a practical consideration for women, a shoe that paid homage to the new post-war machine age with its iconic heel of twisted steel.

OPPOSITE An illustration of exquisite shoe styles by Perugia: on the left red-and-gold shoes are worn with a white spaghetti-strapped dress; on the right purple-and-pink T-bar shoes complement a low-cut tubular dress with pleated side vents. From the *Gazette du Bon Ton*, 1924.

LEFT From top to bottom: the calligraphic Perugia label from 1924, a detail of the cross-strap from the shoe bottom left, and the Perugia *griffe* from 1925.

BELOW, CLOCKWISE FROM RIGHT A satin square-toed mule with cord detail, circa 1925; a black-and-beige leather shoe with woven strap, 1924; and a cutaway double-buttoned black leather shoe, circa 1923, all by Perugia.

The Bottiers of Paris

By the end of the 1920s, due to the devalued franc, Paris was host to thousands of overseas customers ready to spend their money on fashion. They were drawn to a city that had a number of exclusive *bottiers* (shoemakers) whose names have all but disappeared today, save for an artfully inscribed name inside a vintage shoe. A Gillet, the Armenian émigré Sarkis del Balian, and Julienne, one of the few female footwear designers of this period, produced outstanding shoes, and a pair by Alfred Argence or Charles Hellstern were the dream of many a fashionista.

Hellstern was name-checked in the novels of both Nancy Mitford and F Scott Fitzgerald and if a flapper had money to burn, this particular shoe emporium was where she would go to salivate over their silver kid slippers and blood-red suede bar shoes. The firm had been founded in 1870 by Louis Hellstern but

underwent a dramatic transformation when the reins were taken up by his sons Maurice, Charles and Henri Hellstern in 1920. Under their directorship, designs became extravagant, dramatic and occasionally luridly extreme. Hellstern's silhouettes were standard 1920s fare but the use of colour and decoration was sublime. Bar shoes could be of the deepest navy-blue velvet, fringed with steel and sparkling with beadwork. Heels could be celluloid or covered with a searing apple-green suede to deliberately contrast with bright gold leather uppers. Buttons were rhinestone-studded, and buckles were bedecked with pearls or took the form of huge velvet rosettes. And mistresses caused consternation when staggering around the boudoir in a pair of their 'specialist' black-leather fetish boots with 25-cm (10-inch) heels and a thick platform sole emblazoned with rhinestones.

OPPOSITE Hellstern's trademark deluxe satin pumps with an enamel-and-rhinestone Art Deco buckle and Louis heels. The high-cut vamp encloses the foot.

BELOW A pair of soft flesh-pink slippers by Hellstern, circa 1910. Founded in 1870, Hellstern's 1920s shoe shapes were typical of the period but their colour and decoration was exemplary.

▾ Spectator shoes

A popular from of day shoe for the 1920s woman of fashion. Like male correspondent shoes, they came in two tones and were derived from the Oxford brogue. This pair are worn in the fashionable French resort of Deauville in 1923 with a simple linen drop-waisted dress.

▸ Metallic shoes

The fashion for metallics really took off in the 1920s as dancing cheek to cheek in nightclubs became de rigueur. Here, an evening bar shoe in silver kidskin is worn with a fur-trimmed wrap fashioned from a simple length of heavily embroidered fabric and an Egyptian influenced dress, circa 1928.

Key looks of the decade

1920s

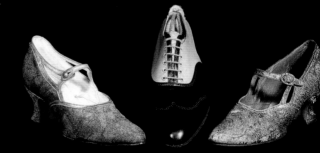

▴ Brocade and bars

Brocade, a heavy weight of woven fabric with an ornate raised design, was a popular fad. It was hard-wearing but maintained an air of luxury and was used in many a pair of bar-strap shoes. Here two pairs of women's metallic brocade bar shoes bookend a pair of men's two-tone Oxfords, all from the early 1920s.

▶ The laced Oxford

The Oxford was low cut with an open or closed tab and three or more lace-holes. Originally derived from the men's Oxford, it was a popular day shoe. The lace-up women's Oxford, shown here with brogue detailing, has a high Cuban heel and arch to add femininity to a masculine style. This 1923 version would have made an excellent walking shoe.

▶ Jewelled decoration

Ladies' evening shoes were highly decorative, with removable buckles and clasps as well as richly jewelled heels, often rendered in Art Deco designs. The heels become the focal point of the shoe and deliberately courted attention by directing the gaze up a pair of shapely ankles to the delights above.

Extrait de

LA CHAUSSURE FRANÇAISE

▼ The T-bar shoe

A pair of pretty pink-and-gold brocade T-bar shoes in a Cubist-derived Art Deco design, a popular leitmotif of the 1920s. During the middle of the decade strapwork on shoes became highly inventive and elaborate, involving a plethora of cut-out areas across the vamp and ankles. This pair are a rather more minimalist example of the look.

▶ Mary Janes

Simple Mary Janes were standard footwear for the day and most women had at least one pair. This was a perfect shoe shape, being easy to walk in with the low heel and protectively high vamp. Here a model wears them with a Russian Constructivist-inspired drop-waisted dress with matching jacket and cloche hat, circa 1925.

1930–47:
The Hollywood Heel

The stock market crash of 1929 and the ensuing economic depression transformed America into a two-tiered nation – those with money and those who had nothing – and many were forced to leave their homes in the heartlands to search for work. The rise of Hitler in Europe presaged an apocalyptic future that was radically to change global culture. Many sought solace in the glamorous imagery flickering across the silver screen of the local picture house as the popularity of Hollywood movies provided an escape from the harsh realities of day-to-day life.

Film stars became the new celebrities and Jean Harlow was the epitome of the Hollywood idol, a blonde bombshell reputed to sleep each night in a bed that was a replica of the scallop shell in Botticelli's 'Birth of Venus'. She was a shimmering figure of fantasy in her white satin bias-cut gowns, created by famed Hollywood designer Adrian. This look had been imported from Paris after the Hays code of the early 1930s forbade 'indecent or undue exposure' in film, with a ban on the naked body – even a show of cleavage was taboo.

Adrian's erotic designs were based on the work of Parisian couturière Madeleine Vionnet, who specialized in gowns cut in the round that hugged the curves of the female body. A little more fleshiness was de rigueur after the lean geometry of the 1920s, and the waistline was restored to its natural place. Silk, satin and crepe-de-chine dresses clung so tightly to a woman's contours that specialized underwear was a necessity, cut on the bias in flesh-coloured silk. In the film *Platinum Blonde* (1931), Harlow, with hair of an luminescent white, posed in a plush boudoir swathed in white fur and a cire satin gown complete with Art Deco diamond clips. On her feet were satin mules; high-heeled and backless, they were the footwear many women were to recognize as the ultimate shoes for seduction. Slinking across a polished marble floor, in a pair of marabou-trimmed mules, Jean Harlow was the new arbiter of style.

New Glamour

As the 1930s progressed, women across the whole social spectrum were able to buy into this new glamour, with the burgeoning beauty industries and increased availability of mass-produced fashion, and they began to develop a real sense of their own identity as consumers. T-straps and bar shoes continued the popularity they had enjoyed in the 1920s and heels became higher and higher, reaching over 7.5 cm (3 inches) by the end of the decade. High-heeled pumps with an assortment of Art Deco clips, and leather brogue Oxfords as worn by Katharine Hepburn, had much rounder toes as the softer shapes of shoes reflected fashion's new curves.

New systems of tanning leather meant a brighter-coloured palette was available, which included visually arresting metallic and pearlized tones. Exotic skins were so popular that in 1932, the Italian fashion magazine *Donna* wrote:

> …*the modern Cinderella exacts contributions for her shoes from the entire planet. From the ruminants to the sharks, from the alligators to the snakes, from the meek goat to the harmless toad, the frog and the lizard of Java. All Noah's ark has been called upon to provide a contribution for the shoes of the modern woman.*

One of the key changes in the 1930s was the increased display of the foot, in particular the toes. New peep-toe and slingback sandals moved from the beach to the dance floor and incorporated transparent vinyl panels that could be etched or decorated with faux gemstones. Seymour Troy, a popular New York shoe designer, used celluloid to create uppers of mock tortoise, which he combined with a soft, pliable navy blue suede. He also embedded diamanté into see-through Lucite heels in a series of shoes, called Troylings, for the younger fashion consumer. Strappy dance sandals with open toes created a latticework of leather that could be spotted on the twinkling feet of Ginger Rogers as she twirled around a film set in the arms of the debonair Fred Astaire.

OVERLEAF A model resting under a glass table displaying evening satin sandals and slippers in a variety of candy colours in 1941. Shoes decorated with bows, rosettes and ribbon work, were designed to be worn for high-society events and reflected an interest in new glamour and femininity.

BELOW In 1935 famed fashion photographer Horst models depicted Moroccan- influenced pointed-toe babouche satin slippers by Barnovi, on the left, and on the right Arabian-style gold kid strappy sandals by Greco.

OPPOSITE By the end of the decade the 1930s shoe shape had changed dramatically from the classic bar shoe – this pair of open-toe metallic evening sandals features high heels and open sides.

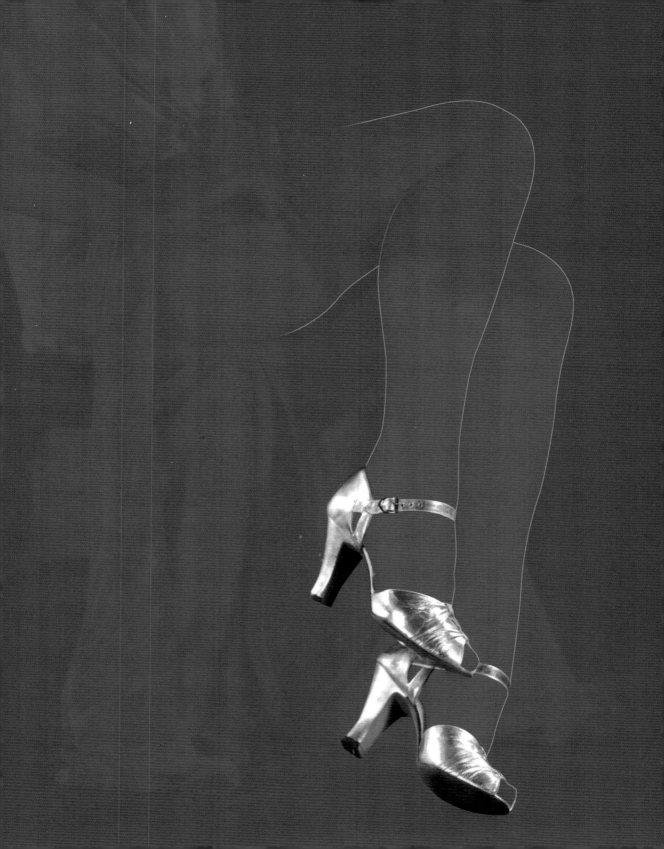

David Evins (1909–92)

The footwear designer most associated with this Golden Age of Hollywood is Englishman David Evins, dubbed 'the King of Pumps' by the fashion press. As a teenager, in 1922, Evins emigrated to America, settling in Brooklyn, New York, where he studied fashion illustration at the Pratt Institute. He left to freelance at American *Vogue* where, while drawing some Delman shoes, he altered the styles to make them 'more interesting'. Herman Delman was furious and Evins was fired for unnecessary 'artistic licence'. After obtaining work as a pattern maker, Evins eventually opened his own studio, producing designs for several manufacturers, and began to promote himself as a high-end shoemaker.

By the mid-1930s, Evins was working with all the major Hollywood film stars. He created a tubular strapped multicoloured pavé wedge sandal for Claudette Colbert in the film *Cleopatra* (1934), and in 1946 made one of the most iconic pairs of movie shoes: Rita Hayworth's platform-heeled black satin slingbacks with ankle straps, worn during the 'strip-tease' scene in *Gilda* (1946). Other customers included the Duchess of Windsor, Ava Gardner, Judy Garland and Marlene Dietrich, for whom he created a pair of leopard-print ankle boots with a pointed toe and brown fur heel. In the 1950s, Grace Kelly, one of his celebrity

customers both on and off the stage, wore a pair of Evins satin slippers for her marriage to Prince Rainier of Monaco, to disguise the fact that she towered over him. In 1948, Evins won a Coty Award for his Shell pump, a court shoe with a very low-cut décolleté vamp that created one of the first examples of 'toe cleavage'.

ABOVE Rita Hayworth in *Gilda* (1946), wearing David Evins black platform ankle-strap shoes.

LEFT A red kidskin and clear vinylite draped evening sandal with front fastening buckle by Newton Elkin, circa 1941.

OPPOSITE Colours became more inventive and dramatic as shown in this ensemble of yellow satin shoes worn with a vivid blue velvet dress and jacket from 1947. Even during wartime, intense colours were used to disguise low-quality leathers and materials.

Shoe Suitability

As more of the foot was displayed, so the fashion and beauty press began to tutor women in how to look after their toes. Magazines carried articles on how to look like the latest star and began to give advice about the most flattering shape of shoe a woman could wear. Lynne Joyce, a popular beauty editor throughout this decade, wrote in 1935 that 'the shoe fashions of today are so numerous and varied that it should not be difficult for the most awkward foot to be suited. A little common sense in the choice of footwear will save a heap of misery'. She advised that women with wide feet should choose shoes with high-built sides, while thin feet should be disguised with plenty of decoration; those with thick ankles should avoid strappy styles and wear Oxfords; and low-cut styles should be avoided if 'they emphasize a knobbly ankle bone'. She counselled that high heels were good for all as they 'braced the ankles and held them taut'.

The economic hardships of the mid 1930s in both Europe and America meant restrictions on the use of leather. Many shoe designers were forced to use more fabric in their designs and a popular version of the Oxford comprised a leather toe and cloth upper which was a much cheaper alternative to the all-leather model. Linen shoes were another chic alternative to hide. Muted colours reflected a more sombre decade, and navy, sage green, grey, rich browns and black were commonplace, but in the evening, glamour held sway as shoes sparkled in combinations of white, gold and silver decorated with sequins, seductive black lace and soft feather trim. By the end of the decade, footwear came in a rainbow of colours: apple green, fuchsia, pillar-box red and deep-blue silks decorated with intricate ribbon work and oversized bows.

OPPOSITE Laced leather shoes with a high vamp from the 1930s, a simple and practical shape that was ideal for daywear and, in this instance, dog-walking.

TOP AND CENTRE A cleverly designed court shoe of 1932 by Perugia in beige leather with a high Louis heel and black interlacings that twist to form a buckle at the front. In close-up, the cutaway front creates a frame for the foot.

RIGHT A streamlined lace-up 1937 day shoe by Perugia that is a study in restrained elegance.

TOP AND CENTRE A 1932 snakeskin and kid Perugia shoe in a subtle combination of black and beige incorporating a chevron (see detail), which was a popular Art Deco-inspired motif.

BELOW AND RIGHT A high-heeled deep fronted court shoe in pearlized leather with gold and silver kidskin geometric decoration (see detail), created by Perugia in 1932.

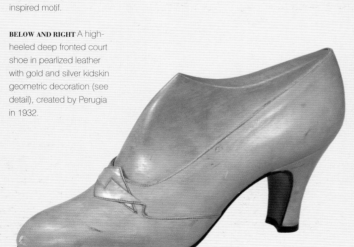

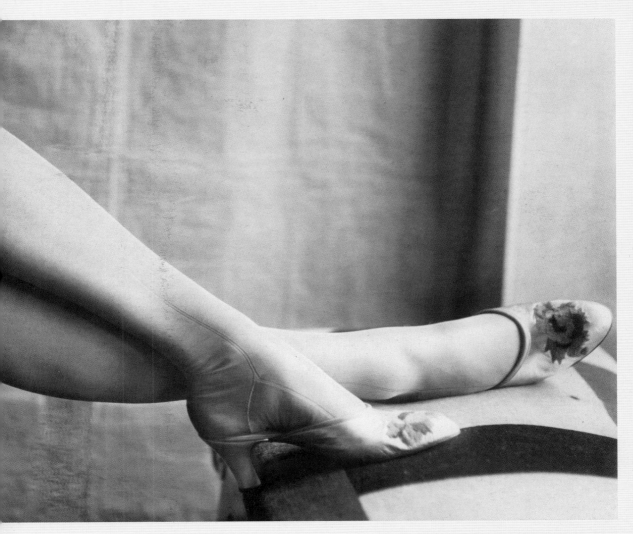

LEFT André Perugia's low-heeled T-bar evening sandal in satin with gold and silver leather inlays and a cutaway vamp from the 1930s.

ABOVE Embroidered silver stack-heeled slippers with embroidered front detail, designed by Perugia in 1935.

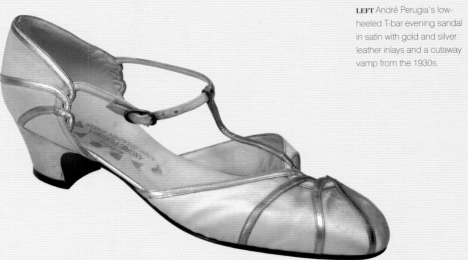

Violet kid and the
new draped heel

Violet and
blue kid.

Gold and silver —
pink kid heel

Kid embroidered with
pink, blue, and silver

Stitched brown kid

Designed by Perugia

Surrealist Shoes

An alternative to Art Deco modernity in the 1920s was Surrealism. This innovative aesthetic had developed in Paris in the 1920s with the work of a group of disparate painters, poets and performance artists, led by the writer and polemicist André Breton. Their project was to study the workings of the human unconscious, the alternative world created when one is asleep, and the resultant dream imagery was plundered for its unexpected juxtapositions of objects.

The neurotic paintings of Salvador Dalí fired up the public's imagination, helped by his imaginative publicity stunts. In 1936, the International Surrealist Exhibition was held in London at the New Burlington Galleries. At the first-night opening, the crush of the crowd was so great that traffic in Piccadilly was left in gridlock and over the next three weeks 40,000 people visited, inspired by the antics of Dalí, who famously gave an address at the gallery dressed in a deep-sea diving suit. He began to suffocate until released with the aid of a spanner.

The highlight of the 1936 exhibition was a living sculpture by Dalí entitled 'The Phantom of Sex Appeal', for which the artist Sheila Legge solemnly glided through the crowded gallery in a skintight white satin gown, her head encased in a wire cage covered with pink paper rosebuds, and a female mannequin's leg in her hand (although Dalí had insisted on a pork chop).

Surrealist imagery invaded fashion in the work of couturière Elsa Schiaparelli, who designed fashion with a deliberately provocative chic-shock appeal for her elegant clients – women of international repute, society beauties and stars of the stage and screen. She experimented with shoes throughout her career, many in collaboration with André Perugia, who occupied the same building as her in the rue de la Paix in Paris. A collaborative effort consisted of a pair of suede shoes with elastic fastenings that could be pulled on and off without the need for buttons or buckles. One of Schiaparelli's most infamous experiments took the shoe from the foot and inverted its meaning by placing it upside down on the head. This amusing Shoe Hat took the form of a black high-heeled court with a shocking-pink velvet heel and was worn by the British socialite Daisy Fellowes. The actual shoe design was based on a popular style created by André Perugia and sold under the Padova label.

In 1938, Perugia showed a thorough understanding of the Surrealist shock aesthetic when he collaborated with Schiaparelli on a pair of custom-made black suede ankle boots that had a bizarre black monkey-fur trim which swept the floor, looking almost like human hair. The original concept came from the infamous 'Le Dejeuner en Fourrure' by artist Meret Oppenheim, a bizarrely tactile fur-covered cup, saucer and tea spoon that turned an everyday domestic item into a sexually explicit object. Perugia's boots had the same overtly fetishist quality.

OPPOSITE A stunning selection of shoes from *Harper's Bazaar* magazine in 1939 show Perugia's astounding range of eclectic influences and daring colour combinations.

ABOVE Four dress shoes with sketches by Padova of Paris for the Elsa Schiaparelli collection of 1937, accompanied by sketches and the tools used in their construction.

BELOW Elsa Schiaparelli's collaboration with Perugia conjured up these infamous black suede and monkey fur ankle boots of 1938, a daring combination of fashion and fetishism.

Salvatore Ferragamo (1898–1960)

The most successful designer to emerge from the 1930s was Salvatore Ferragamo, whose name exists today as a byword for invention allied with the highest Italian craftsmanship. After his apprenticeship to a local shoemaker in his birthplace, Bonito, and an upmarket shoe retailer in nearby Naples, Ferragamo, like so many other young Italians in the early twentieth century, went in search of the American dream. He quite rightly realized that this country's methods of mechanized shoe production were far ahead of Europe's, and to educate himself in all the aspects of the industry and improve his economic prospects, he migrated to New York, where he landed a job at the factory of Queen Quality, a popular footwear brand.

There, Ferragamo immersed himself in American production methods but realized that any factory-produced shoe, however efficiently made, would never reach the incredibly high standards of his hand-crafted version. He also saw that there were few customers in the city who would be prepared to pay the high price of his exclusive artisan shoes. His next step, then, was to move to Santa Barbara, California, in 1914, where he set up an exclusive business specializing in hand-made shoes and repairs for customers associated with the film industry.

In the same year, Ferragamo's hand-wrought designs, which combined exquisitely ornamental forms with function, were discovered by the American Film Corporation. The heroes of its popular Western sagas were shod in Ferragamo boots so comfortable that director Cecil B De Mille was heard to comment, 'The West would have been conquered earlier if they had had boots like these.' Ferragamo's fame spread fast among the movie crowd based in Santa Barbara and his business became a 'shoe shop to the stars', including such clients as Mary Pickford, Pola Negri, Clara Bow and Rudolph Valentino. Gloria Swanson inspired some of his most extravagant fantasies – it was for her that he created his famed corkscrew heels covered with Tahitian pearls.

Ferragamo heels were typically 7.5 cm (3 inches) high and fashioned from wood that was then expertly covered in luscious materials such as gold kid or satin. The actual shape of the heels took many inventive forms: examples include his hollow 'cage' heel of filigree brass and, in 1930, a brass heel in the shape of an upturned pyramid following the trend for Egyptian-inspired imagery that had been popular in the 1920s. His toe design could be equally innovative. For instance, from 1930 to 1935, he experimented with a horn shape – an upturned form akin to the traditional jester toe and based on a design worn in the French court of Louis XV in the eighteenth century.

OPPOSITE A beautifully subtle Ferragamo slingback shoe from 1942–3, hand-woven from polychrome raffia, an ingenious way of responding to the worldwide leather shortage.

TOP LEFT Ferragamo's high-heeled, horn-toed black antelope ankle boots from 1930–5. The exotic black boot is laced with black silk cord and antelope tassels. The collar is padded antelope with a 'presso' closure.

LEFT A stunning black antelope pull-over shoe with painted polka-dots bordered with silk by Salvatore Ferragamo.

BELOW LEFT An extravagantly experimental design by Ferragamo of 1955. This evening sandal of black satin has an interlacing vamp and matching slingback that fastens with a metal buckle. The high stiletto heel takes the form of a hollow brass cage.

BELOW The Invisible shoe, created with nylon thread by Ferragamo in 1947. The F-shaped wooden wedge heel, lined with calf, was a far-seeing idea that has continued to inspire future generations of shoemakers.

Ferragamo was a designer who cared for women's feet and he was aghast at many of his clients' ill-fitting shoes and the lengths they would go to in order to fit into fashionable styles. After studying the bones of the foot in detail at the University of Southern California, he worked out that the anatomy of the human body was such that the whole of its weight was directed onto the arches of the feet. Shoes thus needed to be reinforced in that specific area, and to this end he inserted thin steel plates into the arches of all of his designs so that women's feet always had added support. The toes of his shoes were often comfortably rounded to provide plenty of room for feet to stretch and flex.

Soon the demand for Ferragamo shoes was such that it caused real problems for his business. Unwilling to sacrifice quality for quantity, and finding that American shoe workers could not cope with the demands of skilled production on a larger scale, Ferragamo moved back to Italy in 1927, settling in Florence. The city was home to dozens of small firms specializing in luxury leather goods and possessing the high level of expertise that had been missing in California. Here he established what was to become one of the most famous shoe companies in the twentieth century, making the name of Ferragamo synonymous with Florence and innovative shoe design. Italian shoemakers no longer produced imitations of French couture styles, but were defining an aesthetic all of their own. Combining American techniques of mass production with the craftsmanship of Italian luxury goods, Ferragamo created cutting-edge footwear for the international jet set, in turn establishing his own international reputation.

This fame, and concomitantly that of the Italian shoe industry, was further consolidated in 1947 when he was presented with the prestigious American Neiman Marcus Award, the fashion equivalent of an Oscar. As Ferragamo later put it:

Women must be persuaded that luxury shoes need not be painful to walk in; they must be convinced that it is possible to wear the most refined and exotic footwear because we know how to design a supportive shoe modelled to the shape of the foot. Elegance and comfort are not incompatible, and whoever maintains the contrary simply doesn't know what he is talking about.

OPPOSITE A display of Ferragamo heels, wedges and summer sandals in Florence, Italy, 1947. A concerted effort was being made to position the country as a centre of fashion rather than Fascism after the Second World War.

BOTTOM A bifurcated wedge sandal by Ferragamo with a red suede upper, circa 1935–6. The wood wedge heel is carved and decorated to give a colourful mosaic or stained glass effect.

BELOW A Ferragamo Louis-heel court shoe from 1927 decorated in a gold silk chain stitch. Its simple lines allow such stunning decorative detail.

The Platform Sole

Towards the end of the 1930s, a new style emerged that seemed to break the rules of women's footwear design. It was high, but it was clumpy, and feet no longer looked slim, delicate and small – they had been altered out of all proportion by the platform sole. Many designers claimed to have invented it – Salvatore Ferragamo, Roger Vivier, David Evins and André Perugia – but shoes raised by an elevated platform had existed before.

In the past, the raised shoe had been functional as its height was designed to hold the feet away from roadside mud and city filth, including the contents of chamber pots that were regularly thrown into the street. In rural Europe, elevated footwear took the form of the patten, a sole made out of wood that was held onto the foot by means of leather or cloth bands and functioned as an overshoe. Pattens were so familiar in English cities that in the early nineteenth century, writer Jane Austen evocatively described Bath as full of 'the ceaseless clink of pattens'. They continued to be worn by female labourers right into the 1920s.

The chopine was another form of elevated overshoe popular in the fifteenth and sixteenth centuries in Venice, where wealthy women wore them, some as high as 50 cm (20 inches), as a mark of status rather than for pure functionality. Chopines were so high that a woman had to be wealthy enough to have a servant by her side at all times to prevent her falling; they were also reputed to prevent wayward women from running off for illicit assignations.

By the nineteenth century, the Victorian notion that women's feet had to be small and feminine to be in any way attractive held sway and there was no place for the raised shoe. It was destined to disappear, returning only by the late 1930s. In this decade, the platform sole became a pure fashion item mainly as a result of the work of Salvatore Ferragamo and Roger Vivier.

This new, thick, elevated sole made its first appearance on beach sandals. The 1930s vogue for foreign holidays, cruises and suntanning, as initiated by Coco Chanel in the 1920s, created the demand for fashionable beach ensembles for the wealthy female traveller. Beach sandals were a must and the thick-soled version began to be worn at fashionable European resorts around the mid-1930s. The front part of the shoe was hinged and articulated to make the wooden sole flexible and thus easier to walk in, and gave it a distinctively clumpy appearance.

Ferragamo and Perugia's designs injected a much-needed dose of glamour into the style: a pair Perugia designed for the French film star Arletty in 1938 were in brilliant gold kidskin with multi-straps that included a high buckle at the ankle, and had a cork platform sole covered in gold hide. His black suede scalloped-edge ankle boots for Elsa Schiaparelli in the same year had a heel and platform picked out in a dazzling shocking-pink suede. The actual platform component of the shoe was still relatively low, though – it would take Ferragamo to raise them to more dizzying heights, and in his masterful hands they became dramatic, with exaggerated arches and multilayered soles. The ergonomic of his designs made them relatively easy to walk in, too, as the platform and heel were physically in such balance that the foot seemed hardly elevated.

Ferragamo experimented throughout the 1930s and into the 1940s with a range of platforms in pressed and rounded layers of leather, wood and cork, which were then sculpted and painted, decorated with glass mosaic mirrors or studded with jewels. His most extravagant platforms were made for the film star Judy Garland and are perhaps his most well-known design today. In these extraordinary shoes, the uppers are beautifully crafted out of soft gold kid and fastened with buckled straps, and the cork platform covered in layers of multicoloured chamois leather.

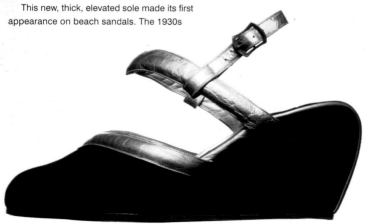

LEFT A 1940 black suede and gold kidskin sandal with a tapering cork wedge heel. Ferragamo usually used cork or hollowed wood for his platform constructions because height could be given to a shoe without it being too heavy.

French-born Roger Vivier, soon to achieve global renown for the exquisite stiletto heels he designed for Christian Dior in the 1950s, also experimented with the platform in 1937. His idea for the style came after a day tramping around Paris in search of inspiration. In a second-hand market he came across a pair of tiny antique Chinese slippers, which he purchased for a few francs. As he put it, 'a close study of these Chinese slippers resulted in my invention of the platform shoe; but my happiness quickly turned to tears because when I sent it to New York I was told it was not nearly dainty enough for American women to wear.'

The American rejection of Vivier's embryonic platform shoe had come from Herman Delman (1895–1955), a manufacturer and high-end retailer of shoes in New York whose business had been in existence since 1919 and had expanded into ready-to-wear in the 1930s. By 1934, the Delman factory was making 2,500 pairs of platforms per week, many of them very glitzy – covered in precious stones, piped with gold and silver and some painted with aluminium to shine in the dark. Customers included Marlene Dietrich, Marilyn Monroe and, in the 1960s, Jackie O. Luckily, Elsa Schiaparelli had a little more foresight and her 1938 collection included a pair of platforms by Perugia with uppers made of jersey fabric dyed brilliant shades of violet and mauve, and a cork sole studded with golden decals in the shape of the sun.

By 1941, platform soles were quite the rage in America and even Delman had conceded defeat and put them in his nationwide chain of stores. Other companies followed suit, such as Joseph Salon, whose Teeter platform was advertised in many popular women's magazines. By this time, many women sought the elegant elevation they gave, and when combined with outfits with shoulder pads by Adrian or Claire McCardell, the look was graceful, tall and athletic. By the end of the Second World War, some platforms were almost 13 cm (5 inches) in height.

LEFT A sumptuous Ferragamo kid sandal with a cork platform wedge lined with red velvet and decorated with hand-embossed brass with rhinestones from 1938–40. The shoe was commissioned by the Maharani of Cooch Behar.

LEFT Ferragamo's most famous platforms designed for Hollywood star Judy Garland in 1938. The shoe consists of a bright gold kidskin upper and a platform in rainbow suede-covered cork.

RIGHT A 1935–6 Ferragamo glass mosaic sandal with a vamp and Roman ankle strap consisting of strips of black satin and gold calfskin. A mosaic of gilded glass is glued to a waxed canvas that covers the cork platform sole.

The War Shoe and the Wedge

Glamour and ornament were eschewed in favour of comfort and practicality in Britain during the war years of 1939 to 1945. A sensible, hard-wearing wool suit was the order of the day for a woman who had to cope with the rigours of rationing – an economy of dress to reflect the economy exacted on her domestic life. Dressy pumps or surrealist decadence had no part to play during this chaotic time and the wedge heel became a common sight, worn with a classic tweedy, hard-wearing utility suit by Digby Morton or Hardy Amies, both British designers.

The wedge heel was invented in the cradle of war as a direct result of Benito Mussolini's invasion of Ethiopia in 1935, in an episode now known as the Italo-Ethiopian War. In response to Ethiopian appeals for help, the League of Nations voted to impose economic sanctions on Italy, which resulted in a severe shortage of good-quality steel. Based in Florence, Salvatore Ferragamo began to find it almost impossible to source the high-quality metal he need for his shoe arches. The imported steel he was forced to use was so poor that when the shoes were tested, they broke. In 1936, in desperation, he invented a new version of the platform heel, in which the space between the platform sole and the heel was entirely filled in. It was made of layers of Sardinian cork so that the sole remained light despite its huge volume and perfectly supported the arch. As Ferragamo described, 'the comfort was in the cork. Rubber would have given a jerky, springy step; cork makes the feet feel as if they are riding on a cushion.'

His innovation was dubbed the wedge shoe, a shoe that was perfect for the woman in wartime who wanted a high heel for glamour but a stable shoe for work. In a pair of wedges, a woman felt fashionable but her foot remained safely balanced – a must in a Europe without much public transport, meaning women had to walk or cycle long distances to work for the war effort. The wedge also gained popularity in America, where restrictions were less acute, and it was imitated, particularly in raffia, by Israel Miller.

OPPOSITE Four women modelling the new Utility fashions in 1942. Glamour was eschewed during the war in favour of simple silhouettes and elegantly functional shoe shapes.

BELOW A pair of women's British Utility slippers in red and yellow felt that date from the early 1940s. The sole is made of a grey composite.

BELOW RIGHT British 'Colleen' Utility shoes by Maceses from the 1940s. This practical style was worn during wartime restrictions.

By 1939, it was estimated by Ferragamo that 86 per cent of women's shoes made in America had wedge heels, and even though he had patented the design in most countries, it would have been impossible to sue every manufacturer. One of the routes to the wedge's success in America lay in an unlikely source: Carmen Miranda, the self-styled Brazilian bombshell also known as the 'Woman in the Tutti Frutti Hat'. Born Maria do Carmo Miranda da Cunha in 1909, Carmen was a celebrated samba singer who had arrived in the US in 1939. By 1943, she was the country's highest-paid entertainer, earning over $200,000 in that year alone. Her Bahian style – part African, part Brazilian – was deliberately designed to make her 1.52-m (5-foot) frame appear larger than life on-screen. Swathed in layers of ruffled, polka-dot patterned fabric, and wearing a towering turban headdress covered in fruit, she strutted the floor in massive sequinned platforms. Many of her shoes were designed by Ted Saval of California, who also cannily produced significantly less extreme versions for entranced American women, eager to experience the new Latin rhythms without the accompanied risk of a broken ankle.

OPPOSITE Carmen Miranda modelling platforms in 1944. As the most popular entertainer in 1940s America, she popularized this towering shoe. Here she displays her extensive shoe collection.

ABOVE RIGHT A pair of open-toed, ankle-strapped, three-tier wedge shoes in metallic leather from 1938.

BELOW RIGHT A 1942–4 Ferragamo oval-toe wedge shoe with a patchwork upper in multicoloured suede squares. The V-shaped vamp is bound in turquoise grosgrain whilst the four-tiered cork wedge heel is covered in strips of blue, yellow, rust and sea-green suede.

Design in Adversity

Although the materials used to create fashionable footwear were severely limited during the war years in Europe, and to a lesser extent in North America after the bombing of Pearl Harbor in 1941, designers took to the restrictions with aplomb. The couturière Schiaparelli was one who refused to be beaten, realizing that creativity could still flourish in adverse conditions. She wittily played with the functional aesthetic of the humble straw basket, carried by the typical French labourer, by elevating it into a must-have high-fashion accessory – and Ferragamo did the same in shoe design, realizing that no matter how cheap the material or how lowly its origins, it could be re-worked into a magical object through true craftsmanship. Straw, plaited raffia, dyed grass, cellophane, even sweet wrappers could be woven to create shoes of great beauty; no real artist could be beaten into an artistic cul-de-sac by austerity and the limits put on the use of materials.

BELOW A pair of high-tiered wedge plaited raffia sandals with a rubber sole, probably made in Italy in the 1940s.

RIGHT A 1942–4 round-toe sandal by Ferragamo consisting of a two-piece crocheted raffia upper in coloured stripes with plaited polychrome raffia laces. The wedge heel is formed out of pressed layers of cork, glued together, with a blue canvas insole edge cover.

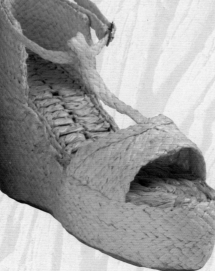

TOP A Ferragamo summer sandal from 1935–6 with a crocheted raffia upper and a plaited raffia ankle strap with raw edged tie. A low heel is formed of four corks sewn together.

SECOND FROM TOP A 1940 Ferragamo sandal made for actress Loretta Young, with a raffia upper and a circular cork wedge heel.

RIGHT A model reclines under a large-brimmed pink sun hat wearing red raffia espadrille sandals in this 1943 photograph.

Thus, Ferragamo showed the full potential of his artistic and experimental side during the war years. The platform and wedge heels, for instance, provided an enormous surface to decorate with chiselling, mirroring and carving techniques, as well as being a blank canvas for hand-painting and mosaics. Wine bottle corks and yarn bobbins were fixed together to create heels, and Bakelite and glass played with the effects of transparency.

In America, a few luxurious materials were still available and in some of the country's more upmarket boutiques, snakeskin shoes could be found even after leather became difficult to source – though only to be worn by wealthy women. In 1942, Laird and Schoeber advertised a range of slingback platforms made out of 'the aristocrat of snakeskin' in dramatic high colours, which included 'batik red', 'jungle gold' and 'parakeet green'.

High slingbacks, where the strap crossed around the back of the heel, were considered very sexy and, by the end of the 1940s, became standard issue for pin-up girls and any film starlet who wanted to suggest a rather naughty image. Throughout the war, many an American aeroplane was painted with the Forces pin-up Betty Grable or a fantasy painting by Alberto Vargas of a girl posed in little more than a pair of slingback shoes.

RIGHT FROM TOP A 1940s black velvet peep-toe slingback with gold-edged bow and stack heel; a gold kidskin and black velvet 1940s slingback; and a British gabardine women's slingback with leather bow, bound in leather, circa 1947.

OPPOSITE By the mid 1930s open-toed sandals became acceptable away from the beach with *Vogue* running a feature on daytime dresses, which included peep-toes and slingbacks, in 1936. However, during the war the peep-toe, regarded as dangerous in wartime factories, was banned, only to re-emerge postwar – as shown here in this 1948 photograph taken by Norman Parkinson for *Vogue* magazine.

Shelley Winters infamously referred to this particular style as 'fuck-me' shoes and recalled how early on in her career, she and her impecunious friend Marilyn Monroe used to steal high-heeled slingbacks from the studio to go out dancing – the most alluring, they found, had bows on the toes and 10-cm (4-inch) heels. The explanation for the rather lurid name was not that they guaranteed a man, but referred to the words that poured forth from Shelley's lips at the end of the night, when the rather tight shoes were finally prized off her aching feet.

For most women, though, utility shoes, spearheaded by the wedge heel designs of Ferragamo, dominated the 1940s until even the designer himself was desperate for a transformation. For him, the typical 1940s shoe had become 'heavy and graceless with points shaped like potatoes and heels like lead'. Diana Vreeland (1906–89), the famed editor of American *Vogue*, also described the shoe of that decade with antipathy:

Everyone was in wooden shoes, clack, clack, clack. You could tell the time of day by the sound of the wooden soles on the pavement. If there was a great storm of them, it meant that it was lunch hour and people were leaving their offices for the restaurants. Then there would be another great clatter when they returned.

By 1947, however, the chunkiness of the 1940s shoe was changing. The use of wooden heels throughout the first half of the twentieth century had meant that heels could be high but they couldn't be thin – since if a wooden heel was too tapered, it would probably eventually snap. This limitation, together with the puritan streak that had, of necessity, entered fashion due to the rigours of war, meant that no real progress was being made in the technology of everyday shoe design. This was to dramatically change in the next decade.

ABOVE LEFT A model wearing simple green pumps by Capezio, worn with a matching sleeveless velveteen dress with a square-neck bodice, 1947.

LEFT By the end of the 1940s, austerity had given way to extravagance and fantastic jewel-like colours were introduced. Shoe, hosiery, bags and gloves were all co-ordinated, as shown in this 1948 selection.

OPPOSITE Towards the end of the decade a leaner, more attenuated silhouette emerged from Paris, displayed in this grey flannel suit by Pauline Trigère of 1948. The length is extended with tapered-heel pumps.

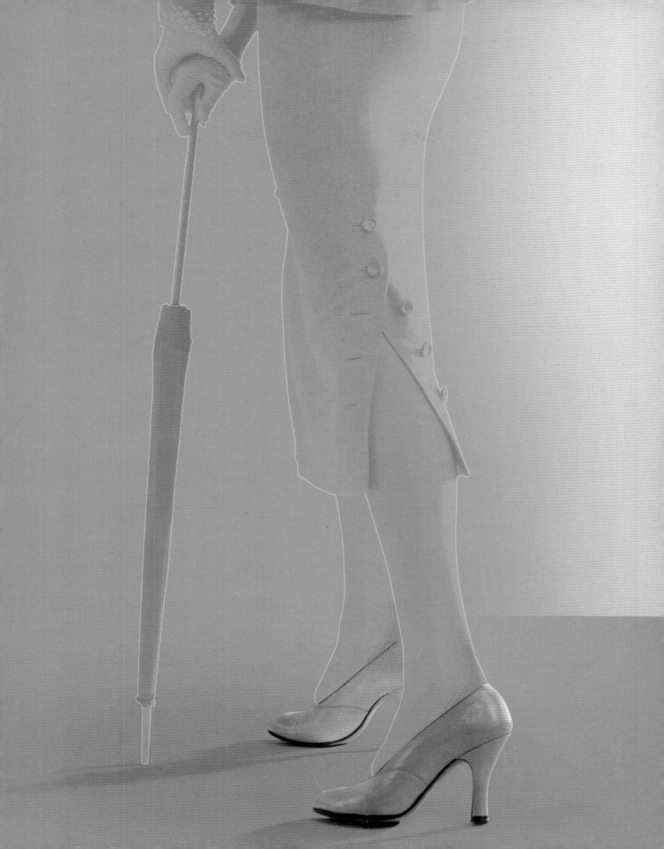

◂ Spectator shoes

Tailored pleated skirts demanded a smart day pump. Here are typical summer day shoes from 1933, clockwise from top left: white buckskin Oxford by Stern's; gingham evening shoe by Shoecraft; brown calf and white buckskin spectator pump by J & T Cousins; patent Peeko Tie with perforations by Walk-Over; spectator sports pump by Florsheim; and white buckskin step-in shoes by Peacock.

▾ Cut-outs and criss-crosses

Cut-out details, cutaways and criss-crossing straps or lacings were popular details in the decade. Here are 1933 offerings, from top: short black leather boot by Bentivegna; satin and leather evening sandal by Greco; and leather evening sandal with interlacing straps by Bentivegna. A Russian high boot by Julienne in black antelope, and long gloves, also in antelope, frame the photograph.

Key looks of the decade

1930-47

Lace-ups

Like spectator shoes, lace-ups were worn during the day and provided a practicality and stability that had been absent in 1920s shoe design. Mimicking menswear, they were conservative with square or round toes with their high vamp they concealed much of the foot. They looked equally smart with skirts or trousers, which were increasingly worn.

▸ T-strap sandals

High-heeled T-bars, especially in satin and often in two or more colours, were worn to accessorize sinuous evening gowns. Here a model wears T-strap sandals with cut-out details by Premier from 1934, with a corded diagonal-stripe silk dinner dress by Rose Clark and stockings by McCallum.

Wood and cork

Clunky designs replaced elegant feminine styles during the day and were made chiefly to wear with street or sports clothes. Primarily due to the wartime lack of leather and ban on rubber, shoes were made with wood and cork soles. Wood never matched the popularity of cork, however, as it proved to be quite heavy. Women strolled the beaches in cork wedged sandals.

Resort sandals

Open-toed sandals, worn at resorts and for leisure, made their way into more mainstream fashions. Here a woman's sandal with striped canvas upper and wooden platform sole, circa 1938, was designed to be worn with a beach outfit of matching jacket, shorts and bathing robe. The front part of the sole is hinged to give flexibility when walking.

Platforms and wedges

Wedges and platforms emerged in the late 1930s, swept into fashion by the Italian designer Salvatore Ferragamo. Initially, the platform shoe was just an elevated sole with the toe lower than the heel of the foot without a distinctive heel. Already seen on beach and resort sandals, the style was brought up to date with modernist details like coloured suede and spool heels.

Deep and vibrant colours

The decade saw every colour of shoe imaginable, including Elsa Schiaparelli's 'shocking pink' and sombre shades such as maroon, black, brown and navy. By the late 1930s, a wider variety of colours was available than ever before. Rainbow colours in suede and satin appeared, but darker, richer colours, with names such as 'fir green', 'havana brown' and 'midnight blue', were also fashionable.

1948–59:

New Look Shoes

The euphoric end of the Second World War meant that the time was ripe for shoe designers to take flight with their imaginations and indulge female consumers desperate for a touch of glamour after the drudgery of war. In Europe, fuel cuts and queuing, soap shortages and rising prices meant that women yearned to be indulged with ballerina skirts, a whimsical hat and a pair of pretty heels. As journalist Ann Scott-James put it, 'As the last guns rumbled and the last all-clear sounded, all the squalor and discomfort and roughness that had seemed fitting for so long began to feel old-fashioned. I wanted to throw the dried eggs out of the window, burn my shabby curtains and wear a Paris hat again. The Amazons, the women in trousers, the good comrades, had had their glorious day. But it was over. Gracious Living beckoned once again.'

First out of the block was Ferragamo, whose invisible sandal was a perfect expression of footwear fantasy. In 1951, Ferragamo innovated again with the gold leather Kimo sandal, which had a satin sock insert that could be swapped to match the colour of an evening dress and was inspired by the traditional Japanese *tabi*, a sandal worn with white cotton socks. The pure minimalism of the invisible shoe and the rather odd-looking Kimo were a little avant-garde for most women's tastes, though, and shoe design was to take a very different form in the 1950s. Footwear manufacturers realized that there was an untapped market for a shoe that completely shrugged off the vestiges of war – as the British trade magazine *Footwear* recognized in 1948, when it declared: 'The heavy, bulky shoe is definitely OUT.'

Consequently, both designers and manufacturers had a very specific goal in mind, which was to preoccupy them for most of the 1950s: that of creating a high, refined and tapered heel that reflected the new Elizabethan age of affluence. Fashions seemed to be veering towards the decidedly more feminine and shoes needed to match.

The New Look

After the war, women were encouraged to abandon their practical wartime roles, devote themselves to their husbands and children and participate in complex beauty rituals – feeling duty-bound to maintain a fixed façade of groomed glamour whatever the time of day. The beauty business began to boom as women began to indulge in all the lipstick, powder and paint that had disappeared during the war, and Parisian couturiers began to reject sturdy Utility shapes in favour of styles that emphasized the bust, waist and hips. Christian Dior's Corolle line of 1947, soon to be branded the New Look by the American press, was an extreme yet spectacular example of this change. His couture designs were romantic and excessive: full crinoline skirts made out of yards and yards of champagne-coloured organza and embroidered tulle, and gowns made of glossy satin or rustling taffeta glinting with mother of pearl. Tailoring was tight, waists wasped, and when the collection was first paraded in front of a global audience of enraptured journalists, it entered the annals of fashion as a defining moment in the history of couture. In the pages of fashion magazine *Harper's Bazaar*, one journalist wrote: 'Paris swells with femininity. The big story is a curving, opulent day silhouette that is the most elegant fashion for decades: a tight, slender bodice narrowing into a tiny waist, below which the skirt bursts into fullness like a flower. There are no angles in this silhouette.'

This frothier version of femininity demanded a new shoe and the wedge was most definitely not it. Consequently, the high-heeled court shoe or pump dominated early 1950s shoe design and was seen as a suitable footwear shape for both day and evening wear. Women delighted in the new Francophile silhouette with its full skirts held out by starched nylon petticoats, and the black suede pumps seen beneath seemed modern and glamorous – the antithesis of wartime utility.

OVERLEAF Coordination was key in the 1950s. Here are a series of five models in the same simple five-button dress of lightweight knitted wool with matching pillbox hats, circa 1959.

LEFT A tweed suit with a draped jacket and pencil skirt by Pierre Cardin, designed for his first womenswear collection in 1957, is paired with black leather stilettos.

RIGHT A crisp New Look silhouette of 1954 by Lanvin, accompanied by the innovative French stiletto heel.

BELOW FROM TOP A Charles Jourdan design for the Séducta label circa 1958–9, in black kid with a rectangular metal motif; a Perugia stiletto circa 1956 in mustard kidskin with intertwined motif on the 'collar'; a 1957 black kid Perugia with a knotted lacing detail; and a 1958 beige city shoe in patent leather with the Brevet Perugia label.

In this new decade, a new vision was necessary, and through the popularity of the work of sculptor Alberto Giacometti, a love of distorted, attenuated forms became the defining aesthetic of the post-war years, a look which had a profound influence on shoe design. This new style took its most exaggerated form in the free-standing sculptural Skylon, as designed by Powell and Moya for the 1951 Festival of Britain, a year-long exhibition on the South Bank of London set up to publicize a regenerated Britain to the world's market. The Skylon played with a thinly tapered shape in the same way that designers began to taper the heel of the fashionable shoe to a gradually sharper and sharper point as the decade progressed. When such high heels were combined with sheer seamed stockings and a tight black sheath dress or pencil skirt, the couture ideal was attained: the look was haughty, svelte and elegantly patrician. By 1950, *Vogue* was describing 'a length of pretty, pretty legs, usually made to seem prettier and more slender because of the high pointed heel' worn under a sheath dress or pencil skirt. The heels created a look of streamlined elegance and length of leg to which all fashionable women of the 1950s aspired.

ABOVE Edward Rayne with a selection of Rayne heels in London, 1957. Once associated with Delman in the US, Rayne also worked with couturiers Hardy Amies, Norman Hartnell, Christian Dior, Jean Muir and Roger Vivier.

LEFT Careful coordinating of clothes and accessories was an essential fashion rule, as seen in these new-season shoes from 1959, worn with stockings and skirts in toning colours. On the right are walnut-brown sandals in calfskin and suede, and on the left basket-woven red opera pumps.

ABOVE The low-heeled pump was a useful day shoe, as worn here in 1952 with a brown shirt and black skirt, both in worsted wool jersey, by Toni Owen.

RIGHT, CLOCKWISE A 1954 I Miller city shoe in blue leather and lizard from 1954 with decorated vamp; a 1954 brown kid I Miller city shoe; and a Séducta city shoe in red with a button-buckle detail from 1954.

LEFT A pair of bright red snakeskin block-heeled city pumps, photographed by Genevieve Naylor in 1955.

Roger Vivier (1907–98)

Roger Vivier is the shoe designer whose name is inextricably linked with French haute couture in the 1950s. He worked with a team of experienced artisans who were hand-picked from the *bottiers* of Europe and included Spanish shoemaker Manuel Mantilla and the Florentine Marguerite Gugliotta. Following in the footsteps of Yanturni and Perugia, Vivier created 'come hither' shoes that were exclusively handmade at high-end prices. For this he was known as the 'Fabergé of Footwear'.

Vivier's career commenced in a small shoe factory when, at the age of 17, he was introduced to the basics of footwear production. This practical instruction in shoe manufacture was then joined with his training as a sculptor at the Ècole des Beaux-Arts in Paris to give him the perfect combination of practice and aesthetics, with which he designed and developed beautiful shoes. In 1937, he opened his first boutique on the rue Royale, where he began designing under his own name producing such idiosyncratic objects as the Surrealist Automatique shoe, which featured an upper decorated with a telephone dial. He also had a lucrative career in freelance design for Herman Delman and Bally of Switzerland.

In 1953, Vivier began a long and fruitful collaboration with Christian Dior, creating a series of captivating shoes that perfectly complemented the dreamy silhouettes of the emerging couturier's New Look gowns. Dior's neo-Victorian bouffant crinoline skirts gave a romantic focal point to the feet, so Vivier began to re-design the basic court shoe shape. He crafted curves into the vamps, tailoring the shoe to fit the foot in the same way as New Look tailoring was cut to fit closely to the body, and his heel designs became increasingly attenuated. The end product was the antithesis of the utilitarian 1940s shoe: a couture shoe intricately cut in satin or leather, bejewelled and as light as a feather. Grace Kelly and *Vogue* editor Diana Vreeland wore his designs, as did Queen Elizabeth II, for whom he designed a pair of gold kidskin shoes with a thin platform sole and heels studded with rubies for her Coronation in 1953. The Empress of Iran regularly ordered 100 pairs of Vivier shoes every year throughout the 1950s, including red satin heels with bows encrusted in diamanté.

Luxurious shoes such as Vivier's could only be afforded by the very few and were perhaps not designed for any real degree of wear. One apocryphal story has a customer returning a pair of beaded pumps to the boutique complaining that they were a little too tight and the beadwork seemed to be on the point of

OPPOSITE Models wearing two elegant low-cut styles of satin evening sandals in 1953 – a black satin pump and a brown satin T-bar.

FAR LEFT Roger Vivier with shoes designed for the couturier Christian Dior in 1954.

LEFT, FROM TOP All shoes Roger Vivier for Dior: a black net evening shoe with tapered heel, 1954; pink silk-satin evening shoe with Rococo-revival beaded embroidery, circa 1958; coral silk pump with coral and diamanté embroidery, 1959; and a cream silk grosgrain pump with coral paste and bronze bead embroidery, circa 1958.

disintegration. The manager was heard to murmur discreetly, 'But, Madame, you walked in these shoes.'

The ornamental extravagance of Vivier's shoes, in particular those embroidered in a Rococo style by Rebe or covered in the iridescent feathers of a bird's plumage, perfectly captured the lure of couture, and Vivier worked with Dior for ten years, his name appearing alongside the couturier's on the shoes' *griffe*, or label. Bold heel designs were his speciality and innovation after innovation came with each heel's name directly referring to its shape. The comma heel was so called because of its flared-out silhouette; his *choc* or 'shock' heel, cast by an engineering firm, slanted away in an inwardly bent arc from the arch of the shoe; the ball heel took the form of a complete sphere, covered in brilliants and speared on the end of a sharp stiletto heel, and was worn by Marlene Dietrich; while the stem heel of 1958 tapered in the middle in a highly stylized version of the classic Louis heel and flared just before it touched the floor. In 1963, Vivier opened his own shoe boutique on rue François Premier in Paris, where his experiments with footwear designs for Yves Saint Laurent were to dominate the look of shoes during the 1960s.

The Stiletto Heel

The exact origins of the stiletto heel in the early 1950s remain murky. By 1952, Vivier was making 10-cm (4-inch) tapered heels, affixing them to classic pumps with pointed toes, and French *Vogue* was using the term 'stiletto' to describe them – but Vivier was not the only designer experimenting with this attenuated shape. André Perugia and Charles Jourdan were preoccupied with heels in France, as were Beth Levine and Herman Delman in the United States and Salvatore Ferragamo in Italy. But Vivier had a distinct advantage over them all: he was working with the world's most talked-about couturier, and the obsessive focus fixed on any product emanating from Dior's atelier meant that Vivier's heels were seen first by the fashion press.

Any shoemaker who had tried to create high tapered heels soon found that there were many problems to address during the process of design development. The traditional heel was made of wood, which meant that if it was to go high it had to be thick, otherwise any weight or strain on the material would put it in danger of snapping. Thus, the tapered heel of the early 1950s was still relatively thick, taking the form of a more refined Louis heel rather than anything radically new. The technology of shoe design had yet to catch up with designers' expectations.

The breakthrough came in Italy as shoemakers began to challenge the dominance of French footwear design, helped by a government campaign to re-brand Italy after the Second World War as less a centre of Mussolini's fascism and more an epicentre of cutting-edge design. Florence was marketed as a fashion city that had the potential to rival Paris and New York, and became synonymous in the public's imagination with *la dolce vita* (the good life) and stylish living.

ABOVE The needle heel of the futuristic Perugia sandal is a 10-cm (4-inch) steel sliver held on by three thin rhinestone bands, 1951.

BELOW A study in monochrome: black-and-white stiletto shoes in 1959, as photographed by John French.

RIGHT A model holds an aluminium-heeled stiletto shoe made with black suede at a show of Dolci's autumn collection held in London, 1956.

By the middle of the decade, Italian shoe designers were taking Vivier's heel designs higher than they had ever been before as they realized that a wooden heel would never achieve the heights that women increasingly demanded. In 1956, at an Italian trade fair, an aluminium metal spigot was displayed – it had been inserted down the shaft of a plastic heel shell, making it much stronger than its wooden equivalent. With this innovation, heels could be ultra thin and highly durable, and by the end of the 1950s, a 12.7-cm (5-inch) heel had become the industry standard. Injection-moulding techniques meant that plastic heels could be manufactured quickly and cheaply and women's demands for skyscraper shoes could at last be met.

The new style of shoe was eagerly embraced by teenagers desperate for a look that they could call their own, one that differed from the staid French couture worshipped by their mothers, and so a myriad of cheap versions with T-straps and buckles, plastic bows and diamanté trim were manufactured by firms such as Dolcis, Brevitt, Lilley & Skinner and Skyscrapers of New York. The Italian starlet look provided a brash, youthful alternative, with its glazed cotton dirndl skirts, bright tight sweaters and hoop earrings – a look that was given a further boost by Marilyn Monroe, who was vociferous in her admiration for Italian shoes. Whenever Marilyn appeared in public it was usually in a pair of one of her vast collection of Ferragamo heels – she was rumoured to have at least 40 – and these were the heels that made her delicious derrière undulate in *The Seven Year Itch* (1955), among many of her much-loved movie moments. According to journalist Jimmy Starr, 'She learned a trick of cutting a quarter of an inch off one heel so that when she walked she would wiggle.'

ABOVE Designer Salvatore Ferragamo discussing a selection of his shoes at a promotion of Italian design in 1953.

BELOW LEFT Ferragamo's Kimo sandal from 1951, with a gold kidskin strap upper and a satin 'kimo' sock. This model was used with clothes by Schubert in the first Italian fashion shows in Florence.

BELOW CENTRE Ferragamo's gold kidskin stiletto worn by Marilyn Monroe in the film *Bus Stop*, directed by Joshua Logan in 1956.

BELOW RIGHT The iconic Ferragamo stiletto worn by Marilyn Monroe in the 1953 movie *Gentlemen Prefer Blondes*. The upper is entirely decorated with red Swarovski rhinestones.

LEFT A chic black outfit gives focus to a pair of red velvet evening heels secured by gold ankle-ties in 1950.

BELOW A high-heeled black patent ankle-strap sandal from Kendal Milne, 1953. Heels became more tapered as the decade progressed.

How to Walk in High Heels

Marilyn's wiggle was much more likely to have come from the increased height of the Italian heel, as it caused women to walk in a completely different way. To balance on such a spindly shoe, women found themselves tilting forwards with their breasts and bottoms jutting outwards and jiggling in a rather salacious fashion. Since having good deportment was a mark of elegance, beauty books began to give advice on how to stand and walk the 'right way' in the new high heels, with ribs high, shoulders down and tummy muscles taut. As Betty Page advised, 'Shoes with heels of the right height, so that you can walk with grace and ease, are in far better taste than the smartest shoes with four-inch heels in which you waddle like a duck.' And Eileen McCarthy wrote, 'Heel heights should be right for you and right for the clothes you're wearing. Moderate heels are best. A short woman in spike heels is as obviously compensation-conscious as a tall woman in flat-heeled shoes. When her heels are too high, a short-legged woman tends to walk stiffly and rivet attention on the lack of length in her leg from knee to heel.'

When stiletto heels were applied to mules, the shoes were particularly hard to walk in or even keep on the feet, as the steep incline of the sole caused the back of the mule to flap haphazardly when walking and to fly off unexpectedly. A solution came with the invention of what became known as the Spring-o-Lator, an elastic and leather insert that ran under the ball of the feet. It kept the sole under tension and pushed up from below to keep the feet in firm contact with the mule's strap. Created by Maxwell Sachs in 1954, this intriguing device was used for the first time in a pair of mules by shoe designer Beth Levine in the same year. Her Magnet mule, so called because the Spring-o-Lator seemed to make the mule stay in place as if magnetized, was fashioned out of black silk crepe and was described by *Glamour* magazine as 'the next thing to no shoe at all'.

Many shoe manufacturers took up the new device in their mule design, including Frederick's of Hollywood, whose Spring-o-Lator Bareback mule – in zebra print, black-and-red patent or Lucite studded with pink rhinestones – was worn by pin-up Bettie Page and dancer Cyd Charisse. The so-called Sweater Girl, a glamour girl whose vital statistics were boosted by a whirlpool-stitched bra under a tight angora sweater, also favoured the Spring-o-Lator mule: Jayne Mansfield posed in a pair wearing a figure-hugging pink sweater and tight leopard-print Capri pants. So ubiquitous was this piece of simple engineering that the all-American girl Barbie was launched in 1959 wearing a pair of Spring-o-Lator mules available in black or brown.

LEFT Black strappy mules with the new Spring-o-Lator, a patented elastic-and-leather inner sole gripping device, 1954.

BELOW LEFT Plastic and metallic leather high-heeled mules with leather Spring-o-Later insole from H&M Rayne, circa 1953.

BELOW Model wearing innovative black nylon net opera-length hose attached to high-heel satin mules by Herbert Levine, 1950.

Winklepickers

By 1959, the stiletto had reached its most extreme height, 15 cm (6 inches) of sharpened steel coated in plastic with an iron tip that could make sparks fly when walking on the asphalt of the pavement. As the heels of shoes became higher, so toes became exaggeratedly pointed, looking like modern reworkings of the fourteenth-century poulaine, a long tapering shoe worn by fashionable men in Europe. The new feminine version (strange for a shoe that has been regarded as a phallic symbol) was nicknamed the 'winklepicker' after the tool used by diners to pick winkles out of their shells.

The overt fetishism of this sleek and sexy look began to provoke comment, for what was the stiletto named after but an Italian dagger used in surprise stealth attacks? The risqué reputation that the style of shoe began to garner was given a further push when disreputable sex bombs such as Jayne Mansfield, Ava Gardner and Lana Turner, known as much for their colourful love lives as their movie roles, began to sport the killer heel. The extreme design of the winklepicker caused much discomfort and led to hammer toes and bunions if the shoes were worn all the time – which was increasingly the case as women ceased to reserve the style for evening functions only.

Older women in particular were ambivalent about wearing too high a heel and not everyone approved. Newspapers began to carry articles railing against this new fashion as a moral panic began to sweep the British nation. In 1960, 'expert' Harry Roberts wrote:

The faults of the conventional female shoe are almost infinite in number… Its absurd general shape, its ridiculous narrowness and exaggerated heels, all are calculated not only to throw all parts of one of our most delicate and important structures out of position, but also to cramp and pinch into a shameless heap the hundreds of sensitive muscles, ligaments, nerves.

He concluded that the stiletto heel was a source of 'potential evil'.

One of the key complaints was that the pressure exerted by a woman's weight on to such a thin heel tip, 100 pounds of pressure per square inch, as some calculated, ruined expensive floors. Owners of country homes, art galleries and museums banned the stiletto heel from their antique parquet and, in 1958, they were blamed for breaking up the tarmac of the roads of Carshalton in Surrey, England. Unusual solutions were found: new forms of armour-plated flooring, myriad different kinds of heel tips and, most bizarrely, the wheel heel design of 1962 by Mehmet Kurdash of Gina Shoes, London. As Kurdash put it, 'This is meant to be a serious alternative to small-based heels which have been banned from dance halls, churches and schools because they damage floors… The disc is set at a critical angle, so that as the wearer puts her foot on it a brake action is achieved. On completion of the walking movement, the disc is given a slight turn, so that a new surface is continually applied as the walker progresses.' The design did not catch on.

For early feminists such as Betty Friedan and Simone de Beauvoir, the stiletto seemed a symbol of women's subjugation by the men who ran the fashion industry – women were so fixated with trying to walk in them that they didn't realize the full extent of their political oppression. As American feminist Karen Durbin wrote, 'Spike heels are combat boots in a sex war where women are the losers.' Many women found the sexual magnetism of the heels too powerful to resist, though, and wearing them became the defining move to female maturity as kitten heels, or trainer heels as they were sometimes referred to, were cast aside in favour of the 10-cm (4-inch) Italian stiletto.

Gina Shoes

The name Gina conjures up an image of glamorous celebrity heels worn on many a red carpet in the 2000s by stars as celebrated as Halle Berry and Nicole Kidman. This British family firm was set up in 1954 under the name Mexico Shoes and at first concentrated on the trend for cork platforms and thick wedge soles that had continued after the war. Around this time, Mehmet Kurdash was approached by a retailer who was overwhelmed by the demand for the stiletto heel from British women and who realized that there was a potentially very lucrative gap in the market. Kurdash responded by adopting an aluminium spigot system, which he set through the centre of a thin wooden heel, and then covered the whole structure in leather. This brave move set the company on the road to incredible success, which was consolidated when the firm was re-named Gina after the voluptuous Italian actress Gina Lollobrigida, a canny marketing move in the midst of Britain's mania for Italian design. From that moment on, inside every Gina shoe the label ran 'Ispirazione Italiana', despite the shoes being manufactured in Dalston, one of the most disadvantaged areas of London.

The company initially produced 70 pairs of shoes per week, a figure that increased to 1,000 per week by the end of the century. In the 2000s, the company is still being driven forward, this time by Mehmet's sons, Attila, Aydin and Altan. Their footwear fantasies appear in the catwalk shows of radical designers Vivienne Westwood, Gareth Pugh and Giles Deacon and feature in countless editions of *Vogue*.

LEFT Gina shoe founder Mehmet Kurdash, far left, with a selection of his shoes at a London shoe fair in the 1960s with his business partner Mr Prezfelder.

RIGHT Black patent leather shoes with an aluminium spigot stiletto heel and pointed toe made for Spencer's of London by Gina in the mid 1950s.

Charles Jourdan (1883–1976)

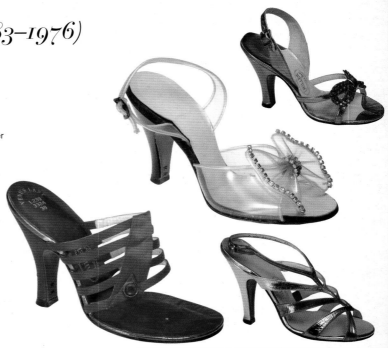

One of the major innovations in 1950s footwear production was the development by couturiers of ready-to-wear shoe lines in tandem with their seasonal bespoke models. Dior saw that money could be made from the new fashion consumer and paved the way with his lucrative partnerships with Vivier in 1955 and Charles Jourdan in 1959. The couturier realized that shoe designs could reach a much wider market than a suit or a dress as they were more affordable and fitted a wider variety of women. Shoes had the potential to make a brand a household name.

Charles Jourdan is a perfect illustration of this, a man who was designing, manufacturing and distributing shoe models for Dior across the world by the end of the 1950s. He had been an independent shoe manufacturer since the 1920s, with his Séducta range introduced in Romans-sur-Isère, France, in 1921. But after the Second World War, his sons Rene, Charles and Roland took over the company and launched a sales office in the Empire State Building in New York and a boutique in Paris in 1957. Their father, Charles, a no-nonsense businessman, realized that some of the qualities of bespoke shoe design such as fit, cut and quality could be easily transposed on to mass-manufactured shoes if the designs were kept simple while still retaining a soignée tailored elegance. He perceived that, to keep costs down, the range of styles on offer had to be kept small, yet if each style of shoe could be bought in a myriad of different colours, three widths and many different sizes, they could be flexible accessories that would match many outfits. A worldwide advertising campaign marketed Jourdan shoes as French high fashion at an affordable price and the label was re-invigorated. Today, Charles Jourdan is a name synonymous with shoes that are good quality, always affordable and not too overtly trend-setting yet with a little bit of couture magic and Parisian chic.

OPPOSITE Every occasion demanded the correct footwear. These 1953 red rhinestone-studded high-heeled opera pumps are from Charles Jourdan, the first shoe designer to place advertisements in high-end fashion magazines, which helped associate his name with haute couture.

CLOCKWISE FROM TOP A red metallic leather slingback with a jewel-encrusted bow by Charles Jourdan for I Miller, 1955; a transparent plastic slingback decorated with metal pearl trim by Charles Jourdan for Séducta, 1955; a glossy kidskin ankle-strapped sandal in red, green and blue by Charles Jourdan for I Miller, 1955; and a red satin multistrapped Spring-o-Lator mule by Charles Jourdan for I Miller, 1956.

SIGNATURE CHARLES JOURDAN ELEMENTS:

+ Understated, classic luxurious ladies shoes with the emphasis on simplicity and quality materials
+ Needle-like stiletto heels
+ Known for the Madly, a block-heeled platform with a high vamp and the Maxime, a low-heeled square-toed court shoe
+ Designed, manufactured and distributed under the labels Christian Dior and, later, Pierre Cardin

Saddle Shoes and Ballet Flats

Outside of mainstream fashion, a new style began to sweep America at the end of the decade. Flat forms of footwear were being worn by fresh-faced teenagers in dance halls, coffee bars and on the university campus. The unisex saddle shoe was one example – practical and provoking little criticizm, it was a style that had been around for years in the form of the sports Oxford and was associated with a sporty outdoor lifestyle.

Beatnik style was a different proposition, though. Spawned by the Beat Generation, a group of disaffected poets, philosophers and novelists headed up by the writer Jack Kerouac and poet Allen Ginsberg, young beatniks were anti-establishment and rejected capitalist materialism – a revolutionary stance that preceded the hippie movement of the 1960s. Beatniks were cool hipsters who read existentialist philosophy, listened to jazz in smoky dive bars, wore black turtle-necks and played the bongos – at least, that was the stereotype. The Hollywood star and fashion icon Audrey Hepburn best exemplifies the look on screen in the film *Funny Face*, which was released in 1957.

By day, Hepburn's character works at a Greenwich Village bookstore; by night, she becomes a jazz aficionado dressed in black Capri pants, white socks and flat shoes, a look that was to be copied by millions of young women who loved its fresh, free spirit and understated chic. On the movie set it was a different story, however, as Hepburn was unsure about how the beatnik look would appear on screen. She was particularly worried about the white socks director Stanley Donen forced her to wear – she felt they would lead all eyes to her over-large feet and detract from the elegance of the all-black beatnik silhouette. Donen was insistent that socks would provide a focus for the movements of her feet in an important dance sequence set in a Left Bank jazz club in which she was to star. She capitulated and after the film was released, she sent an apologetic note: 'You were right about the socks. Love, Audrey.'

Audrey's flat shoes off-screen were by Salvatore Ferragamo, who made her a pair in black suede with a low oval heel and shell sole, an idea taken from the Native American *opanke*, a moccasin with a sole that covered the heel and turned over at the top to become part of the upper. Hepburn also shopped for ballet flats at Capezio, a firm specializing in dance shoes that had been in existence since the turn of the century in New York.

Salvatore Capezio was a native of Muro Lucano, Italy, who had emigrated to America in the 1880s

and opened a cobblers on New York's Broadway and 39th Street. Almost directly opposite him was the Metropolitan Opera House and he found himself repairing a range of theatrical shoes. He became entranced with the complex engineering used in ballet *pointes* and started making his own, which were so beautifully constructed that they were snapped up by prima ballerina Anna Pavlova. Capezio's name was made, and when fashion designer Claire McCardell used the self-same ballet shoes in her collections, they made the transition from dance to fashionable footwear.

By the end of the decade, the ballet flat seemed to presage the youth invasion of fashion that was to follow. Mules and vertiginous heels seemed vulgar and were associated in the public mind with a rather overblown sexuality that was beginning to appear old-fashioned – something had to give. When French superstar Brigitte Bardot was seen in the flat, it seemed just the right height for the 1960s.

ABOVE Peaked Moroccan inspired flat pumps in shiny turquoise patent leather with an overlay of black braid, worn at home with slim Capri trousers in 1951.

OPPOSITE An alternative to the high-heeled 1950s shoe was the low preppy loafer worn by many teenagers. Here a pair of side-buckled driving loafers are worn by model Gretchen Harris, wearing an olive green outfit by Bill Atkinson for Glen of Michigan in 1957.

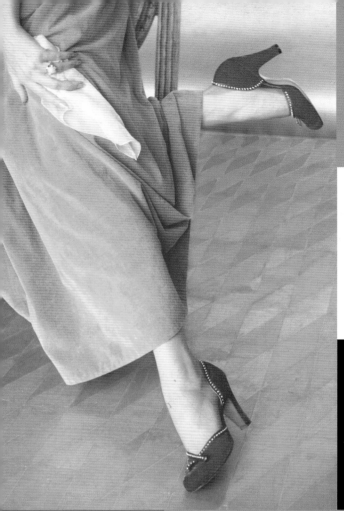

◂ Opera pumps

The opera pump was an expensive, decorative version of the popular court shoe that was worn by most women in the daytime. Opera pumps like this red velvet rhinestone-studded pair by Palter DeLiso were worn at formal evening events.

Key looks of the decade

1948–59

▸ Printed leather

Many day shoes were made in prints to exactly coordinate with outfits, as the woman of fashion wanted a groomed and matched look from head to toe. In this series of high-heeled shoes from 1956, leather is printed with designs that range from abstract through graphic to floral.

▶ Winklepickers

The winklepicker shoe incorporated a long pointed toe that was named after the sharp pin used to pick winkles out of their shells. When the exaggerated toe was accompanied by a stiletto heel, the look was adopted by many teenagers in the late 1950s. This pearlized green leather court shoe with the Lady Orchid trademark was made by Newbold & Burton in 1956.

▼ Strapped sandals

The strapped sandal continued its popularity for evening and perfectly accompanied the fashion for romantically elegant gowns that had been initiated by French couture at the beginning of the decade. T-bars with slingbacks gave the impression of an almost 'nude' foot, as in this 1959 photograph by Horst.

◀ Mules

With the invention of the Spring-o-Lator, mules became much easier to wear as the device acted as a grip and kept the backless shoe on the foot. As a result mules moved from the bedroom to both day- and eveningwear. These stiletto mules are worn with a striped halterneck sundress by Hope Skillman in 1957.

◀ Ballet pumps

The ballet pump or 'flat' became the most iconic teenage shoe of the 1950s when worn by Audrey Hepburn, both on and off screen. It was a fresh 'easy' alternative to the more adult-oriented stiletto. In this 1954 outfit by Capri the shoe is a focal point when worn with cropped three-button Capri trousers.

1960s:

A Youth Revolution

The death of Dior in 1957 seemed symbolic. A new decade was hovering on the horizon and an entirely new attitude to fashionable consumption was on its way, completely divorced from the rigid strictures of French couture. Teenagers began to dictate fashion in a manner that was unprecedented, and the refined chic and structured silhouette of the 1950s was supplanted by the androgynous pre-adolescent body of Twiggy, the decade's fashionable ideal. With her cropped hair courtesy of Leonard Lewis of Mayfair, London, and her short smock dresses by Mary Quant, a new string-limbed coltish look emerged – a look that made the stuffy doyennes of French couture look seriously out of touch. As Quant put it, 'I want relaxed clothes suited to the actions of normal life.'

The miniskirt designed by John Bates was the most memorable visual symbol of the 1960s and, for the first time in fashion, the flash of thigh became an everyday occurrence. The mini gave women so much freedom of movement that they felt released from the body language of adult maturity, a liberation that was expressed in a return to gawky poses and child-like styles. Feet were comfortably placed in flat shoes with round toes and had room to wriggle, instead of being painfully squeezed into the pointed toes of teetering stilettos. The 1920s Mary Jane shoe was revived precisely because of its infantile associations and was worn with thick white stockings and an Empire line jersey mini dress. Twiggy remembers wearing a double-breasted tweed coat 'with puff sleeves like a little girl. And I wore little black patent shoes with little straps across, and plain stockings.' By 1965, the miniskirt had risen to thigh level and tights were worn to prevent the risqué exposure of stocking tops and suspender clips. To avoid any flash of underwear, young women sat with their knees firmly together and their feet set wide apart, a stance that gave a direct focus to the shoe.

From New Look to Now

Hand-crafted shoes in luxurious materials fashioned from the skins of endangered species no longer appealed; teenagers wanted fashion that was cheap and cheerful with its own built-in obsolescence – they didn't care if shoes lasted only a weekend, let alone a season. This throwaway attitude reached its apogee in 1966, when fashion designer Ossie Clark created shift dresses out of paper with floral prints designed by his wife, Celia Birtwell. Throughout the decade, fashions changed so swiftly from mod to space age to hippie chick, that the idea of buying classic clothes in hard-wearing cloth that lasted a lifetime seemed doomed – the move from New Look to 'Now' was complete.

The emergence of the boutique defined the decade and they were the place to find the latest fashions, instead of the grim suburban department stores of the 1950s. In 1955, Mary Quant opened Bazaar on London's Kings Road and queues formed around the block for her pleated pinafores and polka-dot knickerbockers worn with knee socks and slingback kitten heels. This shoe style had been re-invented by Sébastien Massaro for Chanel in 1957, when he designed a simple slingback beige kid pump with a black patent leather toecap and a low thick heel, specifically for the couture consumer who found the stiletto heel a little outré. When a thin but low kitten or Sabrina heel was added by other manufacturers in the early 1960s, it became a popular shoe shape among teenagers including the model Jean Shrimpton, who wore a pair in many of the fashion photographs taken by David Bailey for British *Vogue* in the first half of the decade.

OVERLEAF The ankle boot was a perfect manifestation of the new physicality of 1960s fashion and felt liberating when compared to the 1950s heel. These white leather boots by Hudson were photographed by Norman Parkinson in 1966.

RIGHT A black Mary Jane by Charles Jourdan, 1966, with primary-coloured rainbow detail on heel and toe.

FAR RIGHT A green-and-beige Mary Jane with Cuban heel for Pierre Cardin in 1969.

RIGHT In 1966 Twiggy models the 'Swinging London' look that swept the world – a mini dress and a pair of round-toe red-and-white Mary Janes.

BELOW As skirts became shorter and shorter, moving from mini to micro, both tights and shoes became a focal point. Here a pair of navy-and-white loafers are worn with red, white and blue tights and top in a photograph for *Vogue* in 1968 by Norman Parkinson.

The Pilgrim Pump

Shoes were undergoing a transformation and on 3 March 1961, *Time* magazine was asking, 'Is the winkle picker on the way out?' The article went on to say, 'In Manhattan shoe salons last week, style setters and trend diviners were claiming that the pointed-toe look was slowly becoming old shoe. Offering blessed relief to women, who for five years have painfully squeezed their feet into narrow, stiletto-heeled, pointed-toe shoes, is the radically different "chisel toe" look – long, flattened, square-toed shoes.' The new chisel toe had been introduced by Roger Vivier, closely followed by Edward Rayne and Capezio, who both showed modified blunt toes in their early 1960s collections.

As skirts grew shorter and shoes became flatter, Vivier kept developing new shapes including the most copied design of the 1960s, the Pilgrim pump. In 1965, couturier Yves Saint Laurent completed a series of simple shift dresses decorated with stark black lines and primary-coloured blocks inspired by the paintings of the Dutch abstract artist Piet Mondrian. Saint Laurent asked Vivier to design shoes to accompany the graphic outfits and he came up with a flat pump with a square tapered toe and low heel made out of a new form of artificial leather called Corfam, developed by Dupont in 1962. By deliberately choosing such a slick shiny plastic, Vivier was situating the shoe firmly in the new decade where manmade material was becoming the new deluxe. The focal point of the shoe was a large silver buckle that covered the front of the foot, a modern interpretation of the buckles worn by Puritan pilgrims in the seventeenth century.

The simple, elegant lines and ultra-modern shape of the pump perfectly encapsulated the mood of Saint Laurent's collection – it was also incredibly comfortable to wear and looked equally at home on the feet of a dolly bird or a duchess. In one year alone, Vivier was said to have sole 200,000 pairs with customers including Jackie Onassis, the Duchess of Windsor and Catherine Deneuve, and this new take on French chic was given a further push with the elegant *ennui* displayed by Deneuve in the film *Belle de Jour*, directed by Spanish Surrealist Luis Buñuel in 1967. Cool and sophisticated in her elegant attire – outfits by Saint Laurent, Pilgrim pumps by Vivier – Deneuve takes an erotic journey of self-discovery in her role as Séverine Serizy, a bored bourgeois housewife turned prostitute.

OPPOSITE A model sitting holding a single carnation and wearing a dark brown velvet dress with a linen jabot at the neck by Chester Weinberg. On her feet are white crepe shoes with silver buckles by Charles Jourdan, 1967.

BELOW LEFT Square-heeled black Pilgrim pump with a transparent plastic rectangle inlaid with rhinestones by Roger Vivier for Christian Dior, 1968.

BELOW Silver lurex pump from Bruno Magli's wedding line, 1965. Ornament takes the form of silver metallic stitching and a teardrop-shaped detail studded with Swarovski gems, jet and coloured pearls.

BELOW RIGHT A pink satin shoe by Roger Vivier with a paste-studded band, circa 1965, top, and a yellow silk shoe by Charles Jourdan with diamanté-studded Perspex ball and heel, circa 1965.

The Pilgrim pump went on to be the most imitated shoe shape of the decade and its simple shape was treated as a blank canvas onto which many designers projected their own fantasies. Many pumps were made in shiny patent leather, and the red, white and blue of the Union Jack, now a symbol of Swinging London, was a particularly popular colour combination.

Authentic Vivier pumps were expensive and a little bourgeois, so some teenagers sourced alternative styles of flat shoe. Theatrical tap shoes with Cuban heels, round toes and button bars from Annello and Davide in Drury Lane, London, were a favourite and the company, established in 1922, rose to prominence in 1963, when the Beatles were photographed buying their custom-fit black leather boots with Cuban heels – known thereafter as Beatle boots. When elastic sides were added to make the boots easy to slip on and off, they became a popular unisex style and were given the name Chelsea boots after one of the most fashionable areas of London – the home of the ubiquitous Chelsea Girl, a swinging 1960s chick who dresses in Quant; the name 'Chelsea Girl' was also given to a chain of popular boutiques.

Moya Bowler was another far-sighted shoe designer who made shoes for the boutique collections of British designers Sally Tuffin and Marion Foale. She specialized in flat shoes with short square heels in cream leather or vanilla, blue and plum-coloured suede – colours used way before Biba made them popular in the early 1970s – which were sold in the cutting-edge emporiums of London such as Top Gear, Countdown and Clobber. The signature wide-toe design of Bowler's shoes was referred to as the 'platypus' after the duck bill of the semi-aquatic Australian mammal and was reminiscent of the fifteenth-century Tudor toe shape.

LEFT Round-toe brown pumps with green, tan and beige Art Nouveau-inspired detailing, Gina shoes, 1960s.

OPPOSITE Bright red leather pumps with huge rosette decoration from 1966.

ABOVE TOP A brown calfskin pump with embossed gold leaf detail, Cordalli-Royal label by Gina, 1960s.

ABOVE CENTRE Navy-and-white two-tone patent calfskin sandal, Royal label by Gina, 1960s.

ABOVE BOTTOM Chequer-board pump in gold embossed leather and cream calfskin, square-fronted with a wooden heel and bark-tanned sole, from Gina shoes, 1960s.

RIGHT Red satin stiletto evening shoe with squared toe and a decorative pleated satin flower detail by Roger Vivier for Christian Dior, 1962.

BELOW A split T-bar slingback in gold leather by Roger Vivier for Christian Dior, 1961.

ABOVE An eighteenth-century-inspired evening boot with a needle-thin stiletto heel designed by Roger Vivier for Christian Dior in 1961.

OPPOSITE A presentation for Christian Dior and Roger Vivier shoes for spring 1960. Vivier was the first designer Dior allowed to have alongside his name on the *griffe*.

BELOW A pale pink satin bejewelled shoe by Roger Vivier with his innovative and distinctive comma heel. Vivier was renowned for his experimental heel designs in the 1950s and 1960s.

SIGNATURE ROGER VIVIER ELEMENTS
+ Innovative heels, such as the comma, spool, needle, pyramid, ball, *choc* and escargot
+ Exuberantly jewelled, feathered and embroidered surfaces
+ Sculptural shoe shapes
+ Created lines for Christian Dior, I Miller, Delman, Rayne and Bally of Switzerland
+ Silk satin knee-length boots, outlined in jewels
+ Pilgrim pumps in pastel shades with large buckles
+ Decorated 'collars' on the vamp of shoes

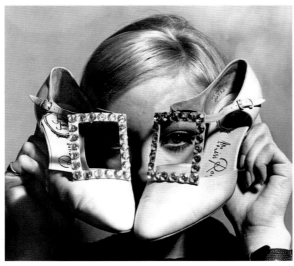

OPPOSITE A model wearing open-vamp white silk pumps with square sequined buckles and a kitten heel by David Evins, worn with an asymmetrical hemline spangled dress by Donald Brooks in 1966.

ABOVE RIGHT Beaded decoration, embroidery and gemstones retained their popularity in the 1960s, particularly for the older, more sophisticated fashion consumer. Here a 1963 Bruno Magli black satin pump has elaborate beaded floral decoration on the tip.

BELOW A range of heel designs from star shoemaker Roger Vivier's 1964 and 1967 collections. From left: a blue velvet with gold embroidery and gems; a curved silver heel on a green satin slingback; and a silver leather pump with a rhinestone pavé globe heel – a feature Vivier used in a smaller ball form to pierce stiletto heels.

ABOVE Vintage black beaded Lily pumps, mid 1960s, with embroidered floral decoration on the upper and heel.

RIGHT A brocaded and gold lamé shoe by Roger Vivier for Christian Dior, 1962, on a beige background decorated with butterflies and flowers, embellished with a double ring motif.

LEFT AND FAR LEFT Cream leather slingback shoes embellished with gem-studded heels and sumptuous velvet bows from the mid 1960s.

Shiny Shoes

The 1960s was also the decade of eye-popping colours: lime greens, fuchsia pink, orange and purple, inspired by pop art, one of the first art movements to have a widespread effect on mainstream fashion. The pop painters were a group of English artists dispirited with the dominance of American abstract expressionism in fine art and included Peter Blake, Paula Rego and sculptor Eduardo Paolozzi. They felt that art should be committed to describing modern post-war life rather than the tortured existentialism of the artist's persona, and in 1956, Richard Hamilton created a visual manifestation of the pop artist's aims in his vital collage 'Just What Is It That Makes Today's Homes So Different, So Appealing?' He assembled visceral imagery from popular culture including film stars, girlie pin-ups, even the brash packaging of the humble supermarket, and rendered it all in artificial, confident, clashing colours.

By the early 1960s, pop art primary colours were combined with the slick shiny surface of the new plastic and PVC (polyvinyl chloride) to become the look that encapsulated the Carnaby Street style of swinging 1960s London. Plastic was perfect for injecting an immediate sense of the future into fashion because it had never been used in clothing design before – therefore, it was almost impossible to use PVC and create nostalgic forms of design.

Fashion designer Mary Quant was the first to use PVC in the clothing she designed for her Wet collection, launched in 1963. Models wore brightly coloured Christopher Robin raincoats with sou'wester hats and matching kitten-heel boots. Her plastic boot experimentation continued in 1965, when she created primary-coloured waterproof ankle boots in injection-moulded transparent plastic lined with cotton jersey in different colourways, so that each shade showed through, and short red vinyl boots with a ring-pull zip. Her trademark daisy logo was moulded into the bottom of the heel so that when walking in the mud, a little trail of Quant trademarks was left behind. Quant recognized the modernity of PVC and pronounced herself entranced by 'this super shiny manmade stuff and its shrieking colours, its gleaming liquorice black, white and ginger'.

Monochromatic hues were another popular fad in footwear, inspired by the black and white abstract paintings of Bridget Riley and Victor Vasarely. From 1961, Riley restricted herself to a simple vocabulary

of abstract shapes including squares, circles, stripes and curves that were combined to create complex fields of vision. Such visual pyrotechnics were perfectly translatable into design details on footwear, and black and white patterns appeared on shoes and boots to give an instant fashionable appeal from early 1965 through to the end of 1966. Riley, however, completely disapproved of this wholesale plundering of her paintings, saying, 'I've yet to see an Op fabric which is wearable. I think they're ugly beyond belief.' Bi-colour combinations other than monochromatic began to creep into footwear design and proved popular because of their immediate impact and visual dynamism. Beth Levine designed daring shoes and boots with the colours dissected vertically, jester-style, into two halves – blue and white or green and yellow (see page 131).

ABOVE Shiny red patent wet-look buckled shoes with block heel photographed by Norman Parkinson for *Vogue* in 1968.

OPPOSITE Op Art influences are seen this monochromatic ensemble from 1964. The black-and-white striped dress and dotted tights are matched with simple black pointed flats.

LEFT Three calf-length boots by Beth and Herbert Levine from 1963 offer a variety of colour, texture and pattern in their styles. Moulded to fit the feminine foot and dyed in brilliant colours, they are, from left to right: a bright blue-and-beige two-tone suede boot; a soft red velvet with gold Moroccan embroidery; and a green-and-orange suede with shocking pink heel.

OPPOSITE Ferragamo suede footwear modelled in 1965: on the right, a yellow suede ankle boot, on the left a blue suede buckled shoe. They are worn with colourful mismatching socks with pompoms and a white-and-yellow sweater mini dress by Micia.

ABOVE LEFT AND RIGHT Model Jackie Johnson with a selection of designer boots in 1967, including the Mary Quant 'Quant-a-Foot' plastic-injection-moulded boots, also pictured in yellow, right.

CENTRE A dark brown suede Ferragamo ankle boot, closed at the back with two buttons, with a low heel and opanke sole (a hard moulded sole turned up around the edge to form part of the upper).

Space Age Styles

As London took centre stage for the world's brightest and boldest fashions, Parisian couturiers realized they needed to re-brand themselves.
André Courrèges, Paco Rabanne, Pierre Cardin and Emmanuel Khan tapped into the vogue for space age style that was proving popular in the plastic furniture of Joe Columbo and polished aluminium and white fibreglass interiors by Verner Panton. Consequently, in 1964, Cardin showed his Space Age collection inspired by the first space walks by Russian cosmonauts, which featured models dressed in futuristic white with helmets, white goggles and flat-heeled boots. In 1965, Khan followed suit with a collection of models wearing silver wigs, silver-soled boots with silver mesh stockings and aluminium necklaces that doubled up as bras.

It was André Courrèges, however, who had the most effect on footwear with his flat-heeled white glacé boots with a bow around the top. In the early 1960s, before Beatle and Chelsea boots were introduced, boots had become very old-fashioned, and top model Twiggy described going 'through whole winters with my legs frozen to the bone because you just wouldn't wear boots… nobody wore boots. Boots meant ankle boots, brown with a zip, the sort of thing old ladies wore.'

Courrèges boots were completely different – his wide flat pull-on, pull-off designs in soft white kid, first shown in his Moon Girl collection of 1964, were modern and comfortable and a show-stopping spectacle of modernity when shown for the first time in his all-white showroom. As the audience sat quietly, a man suddenly jumped from his white plastic cube-shaped seat, stripped down to a pair of white jersey shorts and began gyrating to the beat of tom-toms. Models strode in wearing glittering silver trousers, thigh-high skirts in white and silver and dresses with bonded seams and porthole cut-outs filled in with transparent vinyl. As Courrèges put it, 'It is not logical to walk all day on 3-inch heels. Heels are as absurd as the bound feet of ancient Orientals.'

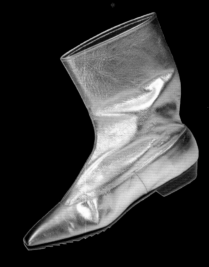

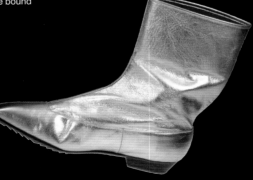

RIGHT 'Space age' gold kidskin boots by Charles Jourdan for Séducta, 1963.

Silver and white were the new black, giving the future a contemporary presence and fitting into fashion like an astronaut into his space capsule. Plastic shoes were no longer for poor girls who couldn't afford leather; the material was celebrated as a modern substance in its own right, appearing in unsubtle, undisguised forms. Thus, the image and status of plastic were transformed by space age designers and became a source of cheap footwear for the fashionable.

The lack of interest that teenagers had for quality and finish in shoes along with the use of plastics meant that factory production could be speeded up. Styles were changing so quickly and the demand for the latest look was so intense that new approaches to manufacturing and selling were needed. Bespoke shoes took too long to make and were too expensive – it was much easier to get the plagiarized version. Courrèges boots were blatantly copied and in the stores in a matter of weeks (the designer was so furious he banned the press from his shows for the next few seasons), and a similar space age style appeared in the store windows of footwear retailers around the world, including in I Magnin, Delman, Ravel, the Dutch brand Sacha and Kurt Geiger. Lotus shoes made a pair of Courrèges-style boots in black PVC with a white trim that were marketed under the name Career Girl.

LEFT Twiggy wearing a fashionable pink full-length coat trimmed in grey fur with bright silver boots in 1966.

LEFT A typically idiosyncratic design by Elsa Schiaparelli from 1960. These unusual theatre boots in white leather with elastic sides have snowball pompoms and crystal heels.

OPPOSITE Gold stretch jongler boots with lilac pompoms and turned-up lilac toes by David Evins, 1965. The model is also wearing black tights with lilac flowers by Bonnie Doon.

Go-Go Boots

Go-Go boots were an American version of the flat Courrèges boot and gained their name because of an association with America's first discotheque, the infamous Whisky a Go-Go, which opened in 1964 in West Hollywood, California, and was immortalized in the song 'Going to a Go-Go' by the Miracles in 1966. At the club, in the intervals between the live bands playing on stage, a female disc jockey dressed in a bra top, miniskirt and flat chisel-toe boots would spin records and dance energetically in a suspended cage – hence the term 'Go-Go dancer'. From then on, any white leather flat-heeled boot that stopped at calf height was known as the Go-Go boot. As the decade progressed, they slowly crept up the calf to become knee-length with elasticized tops by the early 1970s. Cheap white vinyl versions were manufactured all over the world by firms with names such as Golo Boots, College Girl and Battani, and were sold by the American firm Hi Brow, who marketed them 'as worn by the girls on *Hullabaloo*', a TV programme devoted to pop music that was broadcast by NBC from 1965 to 1966.

Kinky Boots

Black leather had been bubbling under the fashion radar since 1960, when Yves Saint Laurent had presented his homage to the beatniks of Left Bank, Paris, in his Beat collection of 1960 for Christian Dior. The black turtleneck sweater was taken from a smoky jazz club and re-interpreted on the catwalk in the finest grade of cashmere; the rebellious black leather jacket was re-made in crocodile skin and lined with mink – and street style was transformed into haute couture. Saint Laurent's collection had caused a furore at the time and alienated Dior's couture customers, but it reflected the changes that were happening in fashion. The fetish element of black leather slowly entered into the mainstream without too much opposition, and one of the first to wear it was Jean Shrimpton, whose boyfriend at the time was fashion photographer David Bailey. On her first trip to America, she wore an all-leather ensemble that consisted of a black leather coat, black leather pinafore dress and black boots which laced up the front and were custom made, a style that was traditionally associated with the underground worlds of fetishist sado-masochism and high-heeled dominatrices.

This saucy look was given further publicity by actress Honor Blackman, who starred in the cult television series *The Avengers* as Cathy Gale, a leather-suited and -booted anthropologist and judo expert who wears knee-length black leather boots with a small heel, designed by Frederick Starke. Boots such as these usually only appeared in the pages of 'specialist' magazines such as *Bizarre*, run by fetish photographer John Willie from 1946 to 1956, and in the work of underground illustrator Eric Stanton – but now they were appearing on British television. In an issue of the *TV Times* in 1963, journalist John Gough wrote:

Honor Blackman manages to cause a sensation even at show business parties. I saw it happen recently. She had come straight from the studios wearing one of her Mrs Cathy Gale outfits from The Avengers, black leather waistcoat over a black sweater, tight black leather trousers and high black leather boots. Aware of the heads turning in her direction, but neither embarrassed by them nor encouraging them, she said: "I'm told leather drives men up the wall. I like wearing it because it feels nice. Off screen? No, of course I wouldn't go shopping in an outfit like this. Apart from anything else, I find boots are too hot except in wintry weather. At home I usually wear a sweater, shirt and slacks." Somebody asked her husband's view of the leather gear. "He thinks it's fun," she said. "He is very well balanced."

Fashion was prepared to flirt with fetishism and kinky knee-length boots; black leather coats and even cat-suits began to be seen on television screens, even at family viewing times; and the naughty origins of the look were acknowledged when black leather boots were christened 'Kinky'. So blasé was the British public over the kinky boot that in 1964, Blackman and her co-star, Patrick Macnee as John Steed, had a top-five hit with the song 'Kinky Boots', which included the immortal lines:

Full length, half length,
Fully fashion calf length,
Brown boots, black boots,
Patent leather jackboots,
Low boots, high boots,
Lovely lanky thigh boot,
We all dig those boots.

BELOW Boots were at their most popular in the 1960s and came in many different styles, such as this yellow leather Puss-in-Boots pair from the later part of the decade.

The Cuissarde Boot

The most extreme manifestation of the black leather boot was the thigh-high cavalier or *cuissarde* style, which covered the expanse of leg that was being exposed by micro-miniskirts. The boots were originally worn in the eighteenth century by the elite cuirassiers or heavy cavalry, so called because of the *cuirass* or heavy metal breast plate the men wore when charging into battle. The heavy leather *cuissarde* boot protected the length of the legs when fighting with infantrymen, and they remain part of many European soldiers' parade ground dress. As a result, cuissarde boots conveyed an image of very potent masculinity, conjuring up images not just of cavaliers, but of musketeers, pirates and all things swashbuckling. A woman in a pair of cuissardes became a powerful image of femininity, and the look was powerfully sexual when combined with a miniskirt – perfect for the increasingly liberated 1960s.

Thus, it was only natural that a designer as experimental as Roger Vivier should be one of the first to start playing with this shape for women, and in 1963, he designed a pair of crocodile cuissarde boots for Yves Saint Laurent's Paris couture collection.

In 1967, French starlet Brigitte Bardot (who had declared that couture was for grandmothers) posed astride a Harley Davidson in a black leather miniskirt and a pair of shiny black vinyl thigh-high boots by Roger Vivier, for a film clip to accompany her rendition of Serge Gainsbourg's song 'Harley Davidson'. She showed the appeal of the cuissarde boot, the way it isolated a strip of bare thigh between the hem of the mini and the top of the boot – which is why it has remained an incredibly popular style whether in or out of fashion. Jane Fonda sported another exotic version of the boots as space chick Barbarella in the 1968 film of the same name – this time they were in white leather, thigh-high and held up by black leather straps that reached right up to the shoulders like a pair of strange braces, created by Italian costume designer Giulio Coltellacci.

ABOVE A collection of flat-heeled winter knee boots designed to accompany clothes by London fashion designers Ossie Clark and Alice Pollock in 1967.

Beth Levine (1914–2006)

By 1966, Nancy Sinatra had written her iconic ode to the Go-Go boot in 'These Boots Are Made For Walking', adding a little fetish frisson with the words: 'And one of these days these boots are gonna walk all over you.' In the film that accompanied her song, she wore a pair of white vinyl boots created by Beth Levine, who designed under her husband Herbert's label. The popularity of the song increased the demand for Levine's boots to such an extent that Saks Fifth Avenue turned a corner of its shoe department into Beth's Bootery.

Beth and her husband, Herbert Levine, were one of the most successful partnerships in footwear history. Born Elizabeth Katz in Patchogue, New York, Beth was the daughter of dairy farmers who had emigrated from Lithuania. She worked as a shoe model for the Manhattan firm Palter DeLiso, whose open-toed evening pumps looked beautiful on her tiny size 4A feet, before becoming a stylist for I Miller, the leading manufacturer, importer and retailer of designer shoes in America. Beth soon became Miller's head designer despite having no formal training in footwear design. In 1944, she met and married journalist-turned-shoe-tycoon Herbert Levine, who realized that her design potential and his business acumen would make the perfect partnership. In 1948, the dynamic duo set up a new company, Herbert Levine, to make shoes that Beth described presciently as 'ones that nobody needed, but everybody wanted'.

Her modern use of materials and her assimilation of witty pop art references struck a chord with customers such as Liza Minnelli, Barbra Streisand and Jackie Kennedy, and she worked with key American designers such as Bill Blass, Halston and Galanos. One witty sandal design had bright green Astroturf lining and yellow plastic dahlias for decoration, while slippers were decorated with sweet wrappers and driving shoes were moulded into the shape of cars. Like many designers of that era, Levine experimented with plastic, creating transparent 'invisible' shoes out of vinyl. Her most notorious design was the 'upperless' shoe, which was exactly that: a sole with a heel and no uppers – it was supposed to stick to the bottom of the foot with glue. Another radical but much more popular design was the stocking boot, a soft boot in stretch fabric or vinyl that pulled on and off like a pair of gloves and had a hard sole on which to walk. The boots clung to the legs like thick tights and were kept in place by loops attached to a belt in the manner of fishermen's waders; they were perfect winterwear when miniskirts were at the height of fashion. Levine also gave an incredible lightness to this form of footwear that was usually heavy – her inventiveness was acknowledged when she won the Coty Award, fashion's equivalent of the Oscar, in 1967.

Time magazine described the stocking boot's assault on New York in 1967 and wrote that: 'On the right pair of legs – ones that are young and slender – the boots can look devastatingly sexy. New York Fashion Plate Betsy Theodoracopulos, who wears her skirts four inches above the knee, says that she likes the high-rise boots because "they give my legs a sleek stocking look, and besides, without them I'd look like an overgrown teenager."' Many designers were caught up with the craze and produced their own versions – including Roger Vivier, who in 1967 created the Ginza thigh boot, with a zipper that went all the way up the inside of the leg, and a stocking boot in brown patent leather in 1968. And these boots weren't just for the young: Hollywood legend Gloria Swanson strode on stage in Los Angeles in a miniskirt suit and shiny black thigh-length boots in 1967, at the age of 68.

OPPOSITE A pair of stocking boots with pompoms on the toes, designed by Beth Levine in 1969. This knee sock-and-boot combination was mass marketed in cheaper versions by many footwear manufacturers in the early 1970s.

BELOW LEFT Nancy Sinatra with her Beth Levine white stiletto boots, made famous by her hit record 'These Boots Are Made For Walking' in 1966.

BELOW CENTRE Beth Levine's upperless shoe, designed in the late 1950s. It has a round toe with a black leather sole, a high-breasted stiletto heel and a sock of black silk satin with two inserts of plastic at the ball and heel. It has no upper straps or closures.

BELOW RIGHT Beth Levine's Astroturf shoe from 1967, one of the subversive and witty shoe designs that show her affinity with Pop Art.

Hippie Hippie Shake

At the end of the 1960s, teenage rebellion took its cues from America and the hippie counterculture developing there in response to a disaffection with the capitalist culture of the world's most powerful country and its occupation of Vietnam. Hippies advocated a return to all things natural, a back-to-the-land aesthetic that was displayed in long, uncombed uncut hair, ethnically inspired clothing, patched and painted jeans and, if not bare feet, then flat earth-bound sandals. The hippie's sandal of choice was the Birkenstock, a functional, practical flip-flop that was first launched in 1964.

Birkenstock had been a family business since 1774, when a cobbler or shoe repair business was registered in Bad Honnef, a town outside Bonn in Germany. In 1897, Konrad Birkenstock designed a revolutionary contoured sole or footbed made out of layers of cork and jute that followed the natural shape of the human foot. The sole was designed to distribute the weight of the body evenly over the entire underside of the foot, and the effect was supposed to evoke the feeling of walking barefoot in the sand. Birkenstock's first footbed shoes were custom made and expensive, but in 1902, factory production was introduced and their price was dramatically reduced. The company was somewhat evangelical about its product and lauded its health benefits, backed up by leading German podiatrists, in training seminars that were held all over Europe in the inter-war years.

The shoe was destined to remain a quirky piece of orthopaedic footwear for outdoors' enthusiasts, but in 1964, Margot Fraser took over as the American distributor of the new Birkenstock sandal and targeted it at liberal professionals based in Berkeley, California – one of the centres of the emerging American hippie movement. Its practical, no-nonsense, anti-fashion look and sustainable cork sole struck a chord with activists and made it the favoured footwear of environmentalists and radical feminists alike. The Birkenstock sandal became a badge of alternative living.

In the 2000s, the Birkenstock was re-branded. A limited edition by supermodel Heidi Klum was wildly successful, American actresses Jennifer Aniston and Gwyneth Paltrow are regularly spotted in Birkenstock Arizonas under their Maharishi combats, and in 2004, French *Vogue* featured a must-have silver pair that had customers waiting in line.

▶ Dance shoes

Twenties-style dance shoes with Cuban heels came back into fashion, such as these worn with a Betsey Johnson dress at her studio in 1966. They suited the more nostalgic forms of fashion that began to permeate into boutiques such as Biba towards the end of the decade.

▲ PVC

A Louis Féraud outfit includes a tweed suit with red piping set off by red plastic boots with a thick rubber sole. PVC (polyvinyl chloride) was the material that encapsulated Swinging London and was first used in fashion by Mary Quant. Its slick shiny surface was combined with primary colours to give a futuristic look that reflected the space age ambitions of the decade.

Key looks of the decade

1960s

▼ Decorative sandals

Supermodel Lauren Hutton wears a pair of Pierre Cardin Turkish pyjamas in 1968. The ethnic theme is continued with the bejewelled sandals. The sandal took over from the high heel as a fashionable evening shoe and its simple outline was given visual appeal with a myriad of different decorative effects.

▲ Cuissarde boots

The highest 1960s boot was the cuissarde, which crept up the thigh and covered all the leg that was being exposed by the short skirt. Their swashbuckling theatrical style suited the more independent and liberated woman of the 1960s and conveyed an image of highly charged sexuality. This skintight pair from 1967 are combined with a metallic mini.

▸ Mary Janes

Top model Jean Shrimpton displays plain round-toed Mary Janes, the perfect choice with minis for that 1960s dolly-bird style. The Mary Jane had been off fashion's radar since the 1920s but enjoyed a revival in the 1960s because of its functionality and youthful associations.

Stack and block heels

be silhouettes in the 1960s were the mplete opposite of the attenuated 50s shape. Sturdy block and cked heels and wider toes gave ch more ease of movement, ecting women's feeling of freedom. s zebra-stripe slingback from nley Philipson and cheetah patent ther pump from Palter DeLiso, 39, show the dominant shoe shape he decade.

Kitten heels

he 1950s the kitten heel was arded as the 'starter' shoe for teenager who was supposed to ove up to full-blown high heels. In e early 1960s its simple shape was mbined with a pointed toe and rted the slow fade to the flat styles t were so popular throughout decade. For many they were a kier alternative to the flat-heeled grim pump. This red leather pair by arles Jourdan date from 1962.

▸ Pointed flats

The winklepicker toe was combined with the flatness of the ballet pump in the early 1960s to create a hybrid – the flat-heeled pointed-toe flat. When worn with minis, it toned down the overt sexiness. This simple shoe shape gave a girlish look that fitted in with the dolly-bird look that was being popularized by models such as Twiggy.

1970s:

Biba and Beyond

In fashion terms, the 1970s is one of the most tumultuous of decades. A woman of fashion could choose to put on a pair of glam glitter platforms and a feather boa, a halterneck dress and a pair of silver disco stilettos or pierce her cheek with a safety pin and pogo in a pair of black vinyl fetish boots – all in the space of ten years. The beginning of the decade was a little more subtle though, marked by the last gasp of the hippie movement as it moved from being a political community that expressed dissention in shabby 'poverty chic' style clothing to a way of marketing deluxe design to couture customers.

In Britian, Ossie Clark, Zandra Rhodes and Thea Porter's exquisitely printed chiffon and crepe maxi dresses had hems that swished the ground and covered the feet, so for a brief time shoes became less of a focal point than they had been in previous decades. The barefoot look worked for festival dressing, but in the city, heavy wooden clogs clip-clopped along the pavements and were worn with an Edwardian-style flower-print Laura Ashley dress and a satchel bag by Roger Saul at Mulberry.

A more extravagantly theatrical look could be seen on the streets by fans of glam rock, and followers of singer David Bowie cut their hair into his signature spiky red style as styled by Susie Fossey and copied his androgynous stage outfits designed by Kansai Yamamoto. Bowie's thin androgynous body was given even more height with a pair of towering platform heels as he strutted the stage as his alter ego Aladdin Sane, presenting a new image of masculinity that was glamorously decadent. Teenagers bought into his look and the glam glitter platform was a shoe that successfully straddled both ends of the market in the early 1970s. It could be expensively deluxe when designed by Terry de Havilland in metallic python skin and worn by Cher, or manufactured out of cheap and cheerful plastic when bought on the high street.

The Wooden Clog and the Espadrille

The clog was a popular choice because it seemed an authentic form of footwear. Wearing a pair made one stylish without being an overt fashion victim, and their lack of any overtly seductive qualities fitted well with the burgeoning feminist movement. Clogs were clearly politically correct because their origins were lowly: they were a traditional working shoe from northern Europe, carved from a single piece of birch, beech or willow wood. They were virtually indestructible, hard-wearing and protective. The rigidity of the original clog also made it uncomfortable, however, so it was usually worn with heavy woollen socks, or the ends and sides were stuffed with straw.

The clog was first touted as a fashion item during the 1940s, when leather shortages in Europe made wearing a pair a practical solution for work in the munitions factories, but they failed to shake off their association with working-class poverty and remained utilitarian rather than fashionable. One unsubstantiated story describes black marketeers wearing clogs with soles affixed the wrong way round so that their footprints appeared to be going in the opposite direction – making it impossible to track such clog-wearing criminals from the scene of a crime.

In the early 1970s, the traditional clog transformed into a fashion item and the shoe developed a less utilitarian and more stylish appearance, either with the wooden uppers brightly coloured, covered in psychedelic patterns in acid hues, or with an added chunky heel and platform sole. When such fashion elements were added, the popularity of the clog increased, growing to epidemic proportions when 1970s super-group Abba appeared on-stage in white polyester jumpsuits and gold lamé clogs and launched their own line with the group's logo stamped on the outside of the soles. In 1978, the brand Candie's took off and their wooden high-heeled clogs and slide mules became one of the biggest-selling styles in America. After a few years in the doldrums, Candie's were recently relaunched with a global advertising campaign featuring actress Hayden Panettiere and a new range of cork wedge sandals and heart-embossed pastel pink slides.

A similar 1970s transformation affected the espadrille, a traditional peasant shoe made in Catalonia, Spain. Rural rope-soled sandals with canvas uppers had been manufactured in small-scale cottage industries across Catalonia for hundreds of years and specialist espadrille makers still exist today, such as Antiqua Casa Crespo of Madrid (established in 1863) and Espart, which has been operating in the small Spanish town of Balans since 1886. In the early 1970s, André Assous realized there was a market for an all-natural eco-shoe and he introduced Basque espadrilles to America. The shape was given a higher

woven platform to give fashion appeal and 90 cm (3 feet) of cotton braid to criss-cross up the ankle – it was an instant success. Many manufacturers took the espadrille shape and ran with it, and by the mid-1970s it was almost unrecognizable from its traditional origins. Dolci's transformed the shoe with modern materials by injection moulding a 13-cm (5-inch) high wedge out of plastic and finishing it off with bubble-gum-pink plastic uppers.

OVERLEAF Platform shoes heralded the glitter decade, as shown here in a photograph by Norman Parkinson, circa 1970.

LEFT Studded wooden heels derived from the clog; these by Italian designer Valentino are worn by actress Leigh Taylor-Young in 1971.

RIGHT Red tie-up espadrilles with rope soles by Laura Tosato for I Miller, 1971.

BELOW LEFT A calfskin clog sandal with metallic buttons and rubber sole, designed by Bruno Magli in 1970.

BELOW RIGHT Charles Jourdan platform espadrilles in black canvas with red leather trim and laces is from 1975.

ABOVE A selection of shoes from 1973 that look so functional they appear almost orthopaedic. The wide shape of early 1970s shoes reflected the new eco philosophy that had entered fashion as a result of the hippie movement and the publicity afforded the Earth shoe.

OPPOSITE TOP Earth tones in shades of green, gold and rust dominated, as with these bright red-and-green patent leather shoes from Pierre Cardin 1974–75, worn with a multicoloured patterned skirt, blue jacket and green headscarf.

OPPOSITE BOTTOM The traditional rope sole of espadrilles soon became a feature of leather platform shoes. Here orange ankle-strap City Lights Studio shoes for Sacha from 1973 are worn with a Liberty's tana lawn shirtdress.

Natural Materials

Dolci's experiments aside, however, throughout most of the decade, the use of natural rather than space age material predominated, particularly in high-end shoe design, and there was a return to the use of top-quality leather and traditional artisan shapes, such as the riding boot. Other forms of flat footwear were popular, including the Dr Scholl sandal and the Earth shoe – both orthopaedic shoes turned mainstream fashion items because of the health-giving properties they were supposed to provide.

Snakeskin enjoyed a revival, one not seen to such an extent since the 1930s; belts, handbags and boots all bore the stamp of the serpent whether real or simulated. The impetus for this revival had come first from couture: Yves Saint Laurent showed python-printed chiffon dresses in 1970, and in the same year, Jean Muir printed satin with a snakeskin pattern and used it on sensuous blouses and dresses with a 1930s feel. Beth Levine in New York and Terry de Havilland in London created python-skin styles that were worn by Cher, Bette Midler and rock chick Anita Pallenburg.

Biba

Nostalgic fashion had a renaissance after the vogue for the space age and hippie androgyny palled, and Biba was the label that did it the most successfully. The British company, founded by fashion designer Barbara Hulanicki and her husband, Stephen Fitz-Simon, started out as a mail-order business in 1963, opened its first boutique in Abingdon Road, London, in 1964, then two years later moved to larger premises in Kensington Church Street – described by *Time* magazine in 1966 as 'the most In shop for gear, a must scene for any switched-on dolly-bird at least twice a week'. By the beginning of the 1970s, Biba had moved to a huge Art Deco department store, the former Derry and Toms, on the capital's Kensington High Street. This new incarnation of the label was a cinematic fantasy, a store that had its own roof garden complete with pink flamingos and one floor decked out as a Moroccan casbah. On pushing through the doors, women entered an Aladdin's cave full to the brim with designs by Hulanicki, who had successfully tapped into the vogue for vintage fashion that had become a legacy of the hippie years. Her outfits evoked the sultry sirens of Hollywood's golden age, including 1930s-style slinky bias-cut liquid satin or panne velvet evening gowns, which were worn with the newly revived platform shoe covered in Art Deco-style black and silver metallic fabric or a narrow-fitting pair of Victorian revival boots.

Biba's colours were subtle – what Hulanicki famously described as 'dull, sad Auntie colours I had despised in my young day'. They included grey, plum, pale blue, dark prune and mulberry, which looked beautiful when used on a rich suede block-heeled shoe. Burnt-orange leather wedges with criss-cross tie fronts could be bought alongside the ubiquitous Biba boot – worn over the knee, the boot had a high, slightly flared, chunky heel, a broad squared-off toe and suede or canvas that was seamed and darted up the leg to give a skin-tight fit. Once the leg was squeezed in, the boot was fastened with a thick zip. The Biba boot came in a range of colours, including sage, duck-egg blue, old rose and purple, and was so reasonably priced that queues would form in anticipation of the weekly delivery – and fights would break out among desperate teenagers if they felt that the day's supplies would not meet their demands. When this skinny-fit boot was first launched in 1969 over 75,000 pairs were sold in the first three months.

BELOW An androgynous 1920s-inspired shoe style. These two-tone brogues were made by British shoemaker George Cleverly who specialized in exclusive handmade shoes for men. In 1972 he made an exception by making this pair for Twiggy.

LEFT Many early 1970s shoes re-introduced heritage shapes. The traditional moccasin is given a platform and heel by Sergio Rossi in 1972.

RIGHT FROM TOP Shoes with solid square heels and roomy squared-off toes were typical for evening and day as in this selection, all circa 1970: Charles Jordan beige silk slingback with a gold kidskin toe and square heel, and a rectangular diamanté buckle; Christian Dior turquoise fabric slingback with buckle; Christian Dior green satin Cuban heel shoe decorated with silver lacing and pavé balls; an ivory patent leather T-bar with pearl button by Charles Jourdan.

BELOW An ivory patent leather Charles Jourdan shoe with a silver ring decoration, 1970.

LEFT A red silk Christian Dior evening shoe with a square diamanté buckle, long tongue and square block heel, 1970.

The Glitter Kids

The subtlety of Biba styling could not last for ever and it was overtaken by another form of glamour: Glam with a capital G. Glam rock, whose exponents were also known as glitter kids, followed the music of David Bowie, Roxy Music, Marc Bolan, Sweet and the Glitter Band – all performers known for their theatrical way of unisex dressing, sci-fi lyrics and outrageous platform shoes. The look was elongated: long flared trousers with high-button waistbands, and skinny-rib v-neck jumpers in primary colours mixed with silver metallic and glittering star motifs and lightning flashes – a mix of pop art and a camp vision of the future. The shoes were bulky, multicoloured and appliquéd, with huge soles of cork, plastic, rubber or wood and towering heels, and the more extreme designs of Richard Smith could be bought at the popular, if expensive, Chelsea Cobbler. In New York, Henry Behar carved platforms out of wood in his basement on the Lower East Side and they were marketed as Goody Two Shoes, and in 1972, the most notorious platform shoe appeared, designed by Harold Smerling – 10 cm (4 inches) of glass that formed an aquarium for a solitary goldfish.

A cheap and cheerful brand was Kork-Ease, whose sandal was launched in 1953, in Brooklyn, New York, as a 'comfort shoe' because of its combination of super-lightweight cork sole and soft leather straps. By the mid 1970s, in one of those strange alchemical fashion moments, the sandal suddenly caught on and was worn by a whole host of female fans including Bette Midler and fashion designer Betsey Johnson, who admitted to having ten pairs. The classic Kork-Ease had a thick suede-covered cork platform or wedge held to the foot with natural buffed leather criss-crossed straps. This inoffensive, vaguely fashionable shoe managed to leap over counter-cultural barriers and be embraced by thousands of young women irrespective of their musical tastes and fashion allegiances. It could be seen on the feet of the hippie elite, complementing Mexican peasant blouses, maxi skirts and chunky turquoise jewellery, or doing the Hustle on the disco floor. Not everybody was happy about the platform fad, though, and in 1972, the *New York Times* wrote of:

… a new fashion malady afoot these days, the broken-bone syndrome. It's the summertime version of skiing's broken leg and this time it's a direct result of those stilt-like platform shoes that are teetering all over the sidewalks of New York. Dr Monroe Jacobs, president of the Podiatry Association of the State of New York, says that 'the platform shoe is supremely dangerous.' Women could not be put off, though, and continued to wear platforms in one form or another until the end of the decade.

OPPOSITE Red slingback peep-toe shoes with orange platforms from 1970.

LEFT The glam rock look laid an emphasis on shiny futuristic fabrics, which could be worn from top to toe. Hot pants emphasized the legs, which were lengthened to extremes with platform soles in 1972.

BELOW Plaited leather platform slingback sandals, circa 1970.

BOTTOM Silver leather buckle 1970s platforms by John Fluevog for Sacha.

LEFT Appollonia Van Ravenstein, photographed by Norman Parkinson for *Vogue* in 1971 wears elegant high-fashion heels with a platform in a shape many associate with early designs of Manolo Blahnik.

Terry de Havilland (1938–)

The most fantastic 1970s platforms were wrought by the hands of Terry de Havilland – the self-confessed 'rock and roll cobbler' who shod the 1970s with his amazing heels and wedges in pastel-coloured suede and metallic python skin. De Havilland, born Terry Higgins in 1938, came from a shoe-making family; his parents owned Waverley Shoes, an independent shoe manufacturers in the East End of London that produced black market ankle-strapped platform heels in the 1940s and black leather winklepickers in the 1950s. After National Service, Terry decided to become an actor, and with his first wife and child lived in Rome for a year trying to make it in the business. It was here that he witnessed the filming of *La Dolce Vita* by Fellini and, after seeing Anita Ekberg cavorting in the Trevi fountain in a pair of stilettos, became fascinated by this erotic incarnation of cinematic glamour.

In 1960, Terry returned to help out at Waverley Shoes and realized he had an innate talent for shoe design that soon attracted the attention of fashion designer Paul Smith, who at that time was working in Nottingham's premier boutique, The Birdcage. The editor of *Queen* magazine, Annie Traherne, also championed his cause after seeing his sexy confections. In 1969, after changing his name from Higgins to de Havilland, Terry developed his most striking design – the Leyla, a three-tiered wedge sandal in his trademark patchwork snakeskin. It was essentially a modern re-interpretation of one of his father's 1940s designs that he had discovered when clearing the attic. Another shoe designer who gained fame in this decade,

Johnny Moke, bought de Havilland's more outrageous designs to sell in his store, Rowley and Oram, based in Kensington Market, and celebrity customers flocked in, including Bianca Jagger, Britt Ekland and Angie and David Bowie.

Terry's father died in 1970, after being electrocuted in a tragic accident on the factory premises, and he was left to take over the business and support the family. As he explains, 'Suddenly there I was – an East End cobbler. I'd be very surprised if I'd got into this business if my dad hadn't been in it. I grew up watching shoes being made. God knows what I would have become otherwise. It was preordained in a way.'

In 1972, the first de Havilland shop opened on London's Kings Road and was irreverently named Cobblers to the World. Like Biba it was deliberately theatrical, with Art Deco inspired peach mirrored walls, purple velvet boudoir banquettes and a huge chandelier – a style dubbed Venetian Bordello at the time. The shop became a mecca for the glitterati who bought 13-cm (5-inch) wedge shoes with ankle straps in peach, yellow, pistachio and blue snakeskin or silver with a brush verdigris tint, and thigh-high satin-lined black leather boots. The Zebedee shoe of 1979 had a corkscrew heel, two straps in pink leather and a blue lightning flash across the front, and the Chassis shoe was made entirely out of metal and affixed to the foot with a piece of ribbon that threaded under the heel.

By the late 1970s, punk was beginning to displace the wedge and de Havilland went underground with a new company called Kamikaze Shoes that made Gothic black leather footwear complete with metal buckles and skull head decoration, and fetish boots for the Skin 2 crowd – but he never forgot the wedge. In the late 1990s, spurred on by Miu Miu showing wedge designs almost identical to his 1970s originals, and Cher popping by his studio and ordering 13 pairs, he re-launched his own-name brand and created a whole series of wedge shoes for Frost French's lingerie-inspired catwalk collection. The shoes stole the show and de Havilland's towering platforms in metallic leather and peek-a-boo toes transfixed a new generation. Now Sienna Miller and Kate Moss wear his gold and red python skin Bene and Margaux wedges, and troubled chanteuse Amy Winehouse performs in his pop art painted mules. As the designer puts it, 'The rock 'n' roll years have never really gone. My shoes have always appealed to flaunters. They're not for the faint-hearted. That *clitter-clatter, clitter-clatte*r sound they make down the street … That's music, that is.'

LEFT De Havilland's Christie wedge, designed in 1969, was the five-tiered wedge that launched his career. The designer's use of multicoloured python skin became a trademark.

BELOW A black patent mule sandal designed by de Havilland in 1979 reflects the fetishism that had entered fashion as a result of punk rock.

BOTTOM A black suede court shoe with marabou trim references 1930s Hollywood glamour. Designed by Terry de Havilland in 1979.

The Stiletto Renaissance

The clunky, chunky platform shoe was eventually accompanied by its polar opposite, the stiletto, which began to enjoy a short-lived revival in 1973, although it was never as popular as the chunky 1970s block heel. Two designers were in the first wave of the stiletto's re-emergence: Manolo Blahnik and Terry de Havilland. De Havilland showed high-heeled designs in Milan, and designed spike heels for members of the cast of the original 1973 London production of *The Rocky Horror Picture Show* and for an early Zandra Rhodes show. De Havilland also re-introduced the 1950s Spring-o-Lator in a series of sexy mule designs such as the Fiorelli shape, which he still produces today.

In Paris, photographers Helmut Newton, Guy Bourdin and Chris von Wangenheim began creating images of a sophisticated, cocaine-fuelled decadence that began to appear in the pages of French *Vogue* under the editorship of Francine Crescent. Femme fatales, strobe lit with lacquered red lips and a flash of black-seamed stocking top, struck a new pose in clothes that reeked of old-fashioned glamour. Black sequinned jackets and satin pencil skirts were worn with ankle-strapped killer heels and pillbox hats with seductive black veils. The result was high-gloss glamour, and Guy Bourdin captured this ruthless eroticism in a series of edgy iconic images for Charles Jourdan that have left their mark on fashion culture.

Maverick photographer Bourdin single-handedly changed the image of Charles Jourdan from a high-quality but rather staid brand to one of white-hot chic. His advertising campaign quite simply mixed glamour with death; one of the most infamous images reproduced in French *Vogue* in 1975 showed an atmospheric scene of what appears to be a fatal car crash with a pool of blood on a pavement next to a chalk outline of a woman's body. A pair of pale pink strappy wedges are left lying carelessly on the pavement. In another evocative Bourdin image, a pair of high black stilettos on disembodied legs walk a cobbled street while a black Citroen appears waiting to run them down.

The high-heeled shoe in such iconic images re-branded the stiletto heel as less the footwear of a tarty 1950s starlet and more the shoes of a deadly vamp, a woman to be reckoned with rather than a fashion victim – and took stilettos away from the place they had been languishing as a result of feminist attacks. It was a shoe of strength not victimhood, and punk made its fetish power even more overt when it was combined with ripped fishnet tights, rubber miniskirts, studded black leather jackets and lashings of eyeliner. Stilettos were hard to find in many mainstream shoe shops so thrift stores were plundered for 1950s originals until the market caught up and they began to

ABOVE AND BELOW An early 1970s multicoloured hand-ruched, open-sided stiletto court shoe from Gina with a patent leather upper and heel. The fine quality of the leather handiwork and ruching is difficult to achieve with today's animal skins.

be produced in their thousands in neon colours such as ice pink or lime green.

Fashion designer Vivienne Westwood commanded attention with her designer version of the punk street style, and her collections in the late 1970s showed stiletto-heeled pumps in trashy fake leopardskin, and black vinyl killer-heeled boots festooned with chains and mini padlocks. These were taboo shoes, normally only to be spied in the secret fetish underground of London clubs such as Louise's and later the Torture Garden, and when paraded on the streets they caused alarm among parents – were their daughters turning into whip-wielding dominatrices? Well no, they were just using the language of pornographic dressing to shock. Writer Robert Elms remembers going into Westwood's shop Sex on London's Kings Road in 1976 and spying, displayed on a plinth, 'a pair of black bondage boots: ankle-high, pointed with metal plates and spikes sticking up from the uppers. This was the most desirable piece of footwear I'd seen.' By the end of the 1970s, many mainstream manufacturers were adorning black and white stilettos and suede ankle boots with studs and the occasional chain. The rebellious punk aesthetic was quickly swallowed up by the mass market.

BELOW LEFT A selection of inventive heel shapes by Charles Jourdan of Paris appears on this page. Below is a black leather 1979 stiletto heel with a gilded tip fastened by two T-bar straps and decorated with multicoloured diamanté.

BELOW RIGHT A 1979 strappy slingback in blue leather with comma wedge heel in blue and black leather.

ABOVE A gold leather Charles Jourdan sandal with a tied ankle-strap and reflective heel from 1979.

RIGHT A red patent leather Charles Jourdan sandal with black patent cross-over straps from 1977.

Other exciting designs were produced: Andrea Pfister's Mondrian spike-heeled mule of 1974, Walter Steiger's gold leather cowboy boots with a high stiletto heel, Silvia Fiorentina's black satin pump with high criss-cross ribbon lacing and Thea Cadabra's shoes that were walking works of art. Cadabra set up her atelier in 1976 and produced shoes that were three-dimensional sculptures rather than practical forms of footwear. The Dragon shoe was a silver metallic and red leather high-heeled pump with the eyes, nose and ferocious teeth of a dragon at the front, and black and silver metallic scales covering the back. The Cloud-and-Rainbow shoe had a cut-out rainbow that was held over the foot complete with hovering clouds and a lightening flash, and her Rocket shoe had a flaming firework exploding over the front. Her patent leather Maid shoe of 1980 was an exercise in fetishism, playing with the French maid's black dress and starched white apron. The maid's legs form the heel, her bent body becomes a rather saucy upper and her white linen apron drapes over the toe.

ABOVE Vivienne Westwood designs from 1973, the first part of her fashion career, show the retro influence of the early 1970s. The 1940s-style platform is re-interpreted for a new generation.

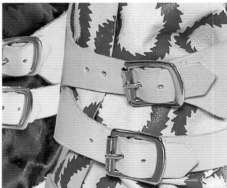

SIGNATURE WESTWOOD ELEMENTS:

+ Influences from fetishwear and punk
+ Curving platforms in bold shapes and extreme stilettos
+ Traditional fabrics used in unexpected ways
+ Multiple bows, buckles, ties and laces
+ Unusual colours and colour combinations

RIGHT Rodolfo Avaro's Naked Lady black patent ankle-strap shoe makes clear the relationship between the high heel and sexual domination. A nude female figure wearing court shoes and long gloves is attached to a vamp throat which forms the T-bar. This one-off design was made by Andy's of London and commissioned by the British Crafts Council in 1978.

BELOW LEFT Thea Cadabra created fantasy heels in the 1970s. Here she presents a cheeky Maid court shoe in monochrome patent leather with a heel sculpted by James Rooke.

BELOW RIGHT Red leather ankle-strap platforms with stiletto heel, circa 1975.

In New York, the rapacious 1970s stiletto became a regular at Studio 54, the infamous disco that opened its doors in 1977 and closed two years later. The club may have been short-lived but it still managed to launch a look that summed up the glamour of this excessive hedonistic age, primarily because it was the haunt of many a member of the International jet-set including artist Andy Warhol, singer Liza Minnelli, celebutante Bianca Jagger and the fashion designer Halston. The use of strobe lights and glitter disco balls made metallics a feature of the Studio 54 style, because of the shimmering light effects they produced when dancing, and rhinestones, diamanté and mirror were used as a way of embellishing strappy shoes. On her birthday in 1977, Bianca Jagger rode into the club on a white horse led by a young Adonis dressed only in gold body paint. For this infamous occasion she chose to wear clothes by the hottest designers around: an off-the-shoulder cream dress by Halston and a pair of stiletto-heeled sandals in gold leather by a young shoe designer named Manolo Blahnik – who was to dominate the next three decades of footwear design.

OPPOSITE A vision of glamour: model Jerry Hall wears gold strappy shoes when photographed by Norman Parkinson in 1973.

RIGHT A Halston puff dress worn with gold strappy sandals in 1978. Halston epitomized the 1970s disco era with his superbly cut and draped designs that were snapped up by the international jet set. Gowns were cut on the bias in silk or jersey worked with feminine curves to create a languorous understated sensuality that was the height of grown-up glamour, and it was this sophisticated hedonism that the brand still evokes today.

Manolo Blahnik (1942–)

Blahnik is one of the most well-known shoe designers today after having been name-checked by fashion fanatic Carrie Bradshaw, the leading character in the popular American television series *Sex and the City*, which ran from 1998 to 2004.
In one memorable scene, Carrie is threatened by a mugger in a New York back alley. 'Please, sir,' she begs, 'You can take my Fendi Baguette, you can take my ring and watch, but don't take my Manolo Blahniks.' Blahnik's name is now ubiquitous, and synonymous with beautiful shoes – but his career really began in the 1970s.

Blahnik was born in Santa Cruz de la Palma in the Canary Islands, which is now a popular tourist destination but in 1942 was better known for its banana plantations. His childhood growing up on the family *finca* (estate) was idyllic, as he describes it: 'Our property had no neighbours apart from my grandfather's house. It was just bananas, the sea and us – a sort of paradise.' His mother had exquisite taste, bought all the latest fashion magazines and regularly flew to Paris to commission clothes from Spanish designer Balenciaga or ordered direct from the Galerie Lafayette. She had a passion for shoes, and if none were available on the island she made them herself, carving the soles from the wood of a lemon tree in their garden and adding fabric straps.

After studying literature and architecture at the University of Geneva, Blahnik arrived in London in the early 1970s, where he studied English and worked in Feathers, an avant-garde boutique in Kensington run by Joan Burstein. In 1971, he visited New York with a portfolio of his quirky drawings and, through a letter of introduction from Paloma Picasso, met Diana Vreeland, the editor of American *Vogue*. Vreeland loved his sketches (and the exquisite but ill-fitting Edwardian boots he was wearing) and advised him to take up shoe design. Back in London, he began creating multicoloured men's Oxfords for Zapata, a Chelsea boutique that specialized in high-fashion menswear, but his big breakthrough was in 1972, when he was commissioned by fashion designer Ossie Clark to produce shoes for his spring/summer collection. The two pairs of shoes he came up with were seriously 1970s: open-toed espadrilles in green suede with fake red cherries hanging from ribbons that tied up the to the knee, and electric-blue suede shoes with 18-cm (7-inch) heels made of rubber – unfortunately designed without a support, so the heels buckled when the models walked down the catwalk.

After this debacle, Blahnik was determined never again to be let down by his lack of technical expertise and began a long study of the traditional craft of shoe-making by visiting traditional craftsmen in the East

BELOW The Brick, made for the Kansai Yamamoto show in 1971 was fashioned out of cork and covered in patent leather.

BOTTOM The Guge, from 1976–7, was inspired by Frank Lloyd Wright's Solomon R Guggenheim Museum in New York City; this is one of many shoes that highlight Blahnik's love of architecture.

OPPOSITE Manolo Blahnik's illustrations are as iconic as his shoe designs. Here is the Ossie, the original shoe made for Ossie Clark's show in 1971 at the Royal Court Theatre, remade after his death in 1996.

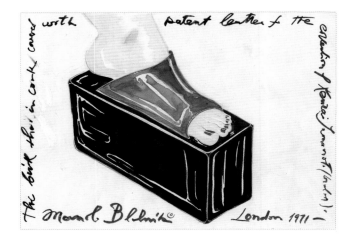

metal wedge (aluminium)

to heel. with cork suri[...]

Manolo Blahnik — winter 79.8'

The gingers. London

End of London and in Northampton, the centre of the shoe industry in England. The rubber shoes were not to be his downfall, however, for their witty good looks had charmed the audience and word began to spread about Blahnik's flair for design. Celebrity customers sought out Zapata and the work of its exciting in-house shoe designer, including Charlotte Rampling and Jane Birkin, two of the hottest actresses of the early 1970s, and Hollywood legend Lauren Bacall.

Blahnik's extreme good looks also helped publicity – in 1974, he was the first man to grace the front cover of British *Vogue* in a photograph by David Bailey, and the furore surrounding him after the Ossie Clark show was such that he bought Zapata outright, with his sister Evangelina as business partner. In 1979, Blahnik opened his first store in America and collaborated with fashion designer Jean Muir (for whom he created a series of gold Louis-heel designs), Perry Ellis and the prestigious department store Bloomingdale's. Customers appreciated his perfectionism and meticulous attention to detail as Blahnik, unlike other designers whose businesses rapidly expanded, still continued to be in complete control of every design that came out of his studio. Even today, he still designs the prototype for every shoe that bears his name, starting from the original sketches (which are artworks in their own right) through to chiselling and sculpting the beech wood lasts on which the shoes are moulded.

Throughout the 1970s, Manolo Blahnik steadfastly ignored one major one trend – the platform shoe. This was a style he detested because he felt that it didn't flatter women's feet, was totally inelegant and thus bore no place in his gallery of favoured shoe shapes. Wide square toes were another no-no, and he concentrated on tapered toes and tapered heels in his work. Towards the end of the 1970s, his shoes became increasingly sensual: paisley boots lined with sable were decorative on the outside, warm and tactile on the inside; red suede stilettos had curled extended tongues; and leopard-print mules and black patent high-heels played with the sense of erotic desire – as well as being technically brilliant jewellery for the feet. Cultural references began to abound in such fairytale footwear, with inspirations coming from a myriad of diverse sources: the Belle Epoque, the paintings of the Spanish master Velàzquez, the surreal films and novels of Jean Cocteau, and the temples of Bali. His eclectic design sensibility and use of materials such as perspex, mother of pearl and coral led to shoes with a perfect balance of aerodynamics, aesthetics and engineering in the haute couture tradition of Roger Vivier and André Perugia – and his shoes were to dominate the 1980s.

OPPOSITE The Gruyère sandal of 1979 was one of Blahnik's first experiments with heel-less shoes.

RIGHT The Piaggi of 1974 was an Op-Art shoe designed for the celebrated fashionista Anna Piaggi, a close friend and collaborator of Manolo Blahnik's.

▲ Stack heels

Early 1970s shoes combined height with chunkiness and continued to use the round wide toe that had dominated the 1960s. The extreme height of the heel was balanced with a platform that made the shoes surprisingly comfortable and relatively easy to walk in.

▸ Denim

The rise and fall of the 1960s hippie movement left a legacy in the 1970s – the craze for denim. Manipulated into many forms, denim was used for dresses, handbags, hats and of course shoes, as in this pair of blue denim ankle-strap platforms manufactured by Dolci's in 1976.

Key looks
of the decade

1970s

▸ Platforms

The platform wedge was all the rage when Martin Scorcese directed *Taxi Driver* in 1976. Jodie Foster wore a red suede pair to give a precocious Lolita edge to her role. Wedges were worn with tiny hotpants to lengthen the leg and exaggerate proportions.

▶ Patchwork

Nostalgia, revivalism and a love of heritage caused many shoe silhouettes and techniques to be revived in this decade. Here a clog shape is combined with patchwork in shoes by Vaccari, Italy, 1976. Patchwork was a handcrafted technique that had been revived by the hippie movement and was applied to jeans, bags and shoes.

Dr Scholls

Scholls were originally designed as functional exercise sandals and had a wooden sole and a beige leather upper in the form of a buckled strap. In the 1970s this orthopaedic shoe made its way into fashion and was worn by many women for style rather than function. This beige leather pair date from 1970.

▶ Clogs

Clogs are a traditional form of working shoe with a wooden sole, worn in many cultures all over the world. In this decade their chunky look entered footwear vocabulary, but the original functionality disappeared when a range of teetering platform soles and chunky heels were added. This extreme pair with towering heels and leather uppers was designed in 1972.

1980s:

Dress for Success

The 1980s was a label-obsessed era: logo-mania was rife and the names to be seen in were Gucci, Louis Vuitton and Hermès – classic fashion houses that re-launched to capitalize on the global economic boom. In this decade of brash excess, newly moneyed 'yuppies' flaunted the brand names of modern multinationals – as long as they had the right aspirational credentials and price tag. Accessories by Ralph Lauren, Gianni Versace and Giorgio Armani provided clear evidence of a successful lifestyle, and their shoes boldly identified their makers.

The classic Gucci loafer was flashed around every chi-chi wine bar and Michelin-starred restaurant: low heeled with a metal snaffle bit across the instep, it became an international status symbol for both men and women. The original woman's loafer, known as Model 360, was modified to have a stacked leather heel embedded with a narrow gold chain and a matching chain strung across the front of the vamp. Customers could choose from several different kinds of leather and colours including pistachio-green pigskin or pale pink lizard. Tod's also produced an equally memorable loafer that took off in the early 1980s: the Gommino was made from soft suede and had distinctive 133 rubber pebbles on the sole and heel.

The long-established fashion house of Chanel underwent a complete re-branding exercise in 1983 and was transformed into a hip young label when Karl Lagerfeld took over as design director. Lagerfeld realized the power of the label's instantly identifiable logos and covered T-shirts, sunglasses, bags and high-heels with Chanel's signature camellia flower, while strappy sandals had the distinctive interlocked Cs inscribed on the front, and quilted biker boots had the Chanel name emblazoned in capital letters.

The shoe consumer who best sums up the overt consumption of the 1980s is Imelda Marcos, First Lady of the Philippines, who had a penchant for the designs of Salvatore Ferragamo during her life of luxury as the wife of President Ferdinand E Marcos. Designers from all over the world were flown to her palace to tempt her with their latest shoe collections and she made regular trips to Harrods in London, Bloomingdale's in New York and the via Condotti in Rome to satisfy her addiction to luxury designer brands. On her flight to exile in 1986, she reputedly left behind 3,000 pairs of designer shoes. Today, her notorious collection forms the basis of the Marikina City Footwear Museum in Manila, which opened in 2001.

Power Shoes

With 'baby boomers' entering positions of power and the role of women in the workplace changing, it was clear that women were achieving more control in society and beginning to storm the bastions of the executive workplace. This had to have an effect on shoes, and arguments abounded about what the newly powerful female boss should wear at work. Feminine frills were out of the question if women wanted to be taken seriously outside of the cosiness of home. Help was at hand when the fashion bible of the decade was published in 1980. John T Molloy's *Women: Dress for Success* was a serious tome that gave information about the use of clothes as a psychological tool to succeed in the workplace. Molloy believed that women had to be taught how to look the part and his heartfelt advice was that they should look sober and serious in dark suits and simple shoes. He wrote:

The best shoe for a businesswoman is the plain pump, in a dark colour, with closed toe and heel. The heel should be about an inch-and-a-half high. The colours that test best for office wear are blue, black, deep brown and grey. One additional note: the towering platform shoe is the most preposterous thing manufactured for women since the chastity belt.

Molloy felt that dress should ignore the trivialities of fashion, hence his antipathy to the platform shoe, and should strive to impart a feeling of power – eventually the new business style he was advocating was dubbed 'power dressing'. Women found Molloy's understated look a bit limiting, though, and as the decade unfolded, dressing for success evolved into a look of brightly coloured, sharply tailored suits with padded shoulders, just-above-the-knee skirts and a pair of heeled pumps by Chanel in tan and black, or red suede stilettos by Charles Jourdan – if one could afford them.

OVERLEAF The white stiletto encapsulated the brash look of the 1980s, here worn with a Katherine Hamnett shift dress in 1987. Black wedge heels with pointed toes are worn on the right.

LEFT High-status dressing from Chanel in 1987, an ensemble completed with the labels' classic monochrome pumps.

BELOW Two-tone Gina shoes from the 1980s in cream kidskin and aqua patent leather with stiletto heels.

LEFT Karl Lagerfeld revitalized the Chanel brand in the 1980s. Here a pair of classic duo-tone day court shoes are worn with a navy blue couture suit in 1983.

BELOW LEFT Robert Clergerie court shoes in black-and-white leather from 1986.

LEFT A multicoloured Gina court shoe and clutch from the 1980s with pink Art Deco revival motif. The vogue for post-modernism in the decade meant that historical detail and vivid colours could be mixed with little regard for traditional notions of taste and understatement. This self-confident look was typical of the decade.

OPPOSITE TOP Toe details on Gina shoes from the 1980s. Highly decorated toes were a feature of the period.

OPPOSITE RIGHT Embellishment took many extravagant forms in the 1980s. Here, red suede Gina shoes have a silver diamanté ribbon detail and silver leaf decoration.

GINA

LEFT AND BELOW LEFT
An advertisement for Gina butterfly shoes, with the grey suede version with silver binding below. A gold-and-diamanté butterfly decorates the back.

OPPOSITE Strappy shoes with tapered heels from 1985.

OPPOSITE, CLOCKWISE A 1980 red satin pump with toe rosette; a 1986 red-print peep-toe with bow decoration and needle heel; and a 1988 blue fabric court shoe with red leather heel and yellow leather decoration, all by Charles Jourdan. Gold leather shoe by Christian Dior, 1987, with black-and-gold honeycomb detail on toe, heel and back.

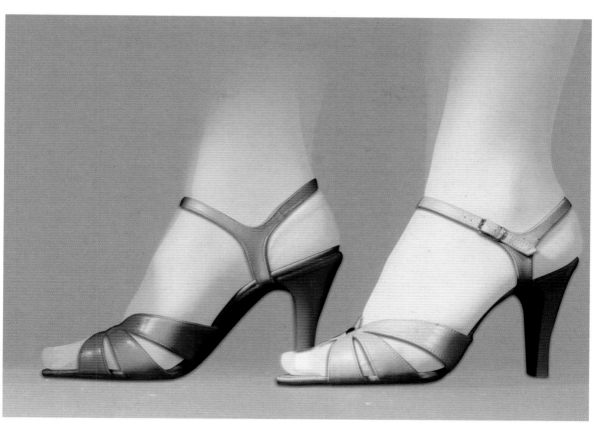

Killer Heels

Discretion was out and there was no such thing as a vulgar designer shoe – and all the better if it had a matching designer bag. High heels dominated the decade after Manolo Blahnik had re-established their reputation as a shoe of glamour rather than tawdry sexuality. The Louis hourglass heel came back into fashion with a vengeance, as did towering spikes – the most lethal were metal spike heels by Thierry Mugler – and a new cone shape, devised by Maud Frizon, that was used by Bruno Magli, Andrea Pfister and Blahnik throughout the decade. The cone heel was literally shaped like a cone, wide at the top and then tapering down to a point, giving it a sturdier yet more futuristic look than a stiletto. Cone heels appeared on Magli's cherry-red suede, peep-toed pumps, Pfister's black leather fishnet slingbacks in a snake and lizard camouflage pattern, and Frizon's pewter and bronze leather cuffed cavalier boots. Pfister wittily played with the heel's name by making it look like a cornet filled with multicoloured ice-cream that appeared to drip down the back of the shoe.

As dramatic hues and oversized silhouettes entered women's wardrobes, neon brights and extravagant embellishment abounded over footwear. A woman could wear a fuchsia-pink padded-shouldered suit with canary-yellow shoes covered in gemstones, or a batwing cocktail dress with a pair of metallic stilettos. Manolo Blahnik remained a key name as more and more women were prepared to spend hundreds of dollars on his much-imitated designer heels, and most of his styles sold out as soon as they launched. In this decade, Blahnik's shoes veered from being simple, stark silhouettes, in which the beauty of the line was crucial, to beaded and braided designs of baroque opulence, such as his Viuda of 1985, an ottoman silk court shoe with a leather ankle strap and pleated point d'esprit lace bib, or the Orientalia of 1986, a mule in antiqued gold-leaf lizardskin covered in pearls, semi-precious stones and beadwork. As he put it, 'What appeals to me about footwear is that you can touch a shoe and play with the materials. But a shoe, above all, is a solid shape. And while what you can do with the basic shape of a heel and sole seems limited, actually the opportunities are infinite.'

Blahnik had many distinguished aficionados including Jerry Hall, the supermodel and consort to Mick Jagger, who accessorized her dramatic Anthony Price gowns with Blahnik's black suede heels and wore his flat gold leather thongs when sunning herself on the beach at Mustique (her penchant for this simple sandal has made her commission exactly the same style for every summer holiday since 1984). American *Vogue* editor Anna Wintour combined couture suits with his sexy reptile-skin shoes and gave rise to the term 'limo heels'. This was used to describe heels that were so high they were nigh-on impossible to walk in – and so the women who wore them effectively paid others to do it for them by having a limousine to ferry them around. If the funds weren't available to have a chauffeur permanently on standby, women took another option – they wore trainers to work and changed into heels when they reached the office, and so the power-suited woman in Nikes became a common sight on the pavements of New York.

BELOW Cone heels in black patent leather and red deerskin by Charles Jourdan, 1983.

TOP RIGHT Killer metal-spike heels from Thierry Mugler's 1988–9 Autumn/Winter collection, worn with black vinyl trousers and shirts. Mugler has exposed the metal spike of the stiletto rather than covering it with leather.

ABOVE Cone heels in gold and black from Missoni in 1982, worn with multicoloured patchwork dresses.

OPPOSITE Stiletto-heeled thigh-high white satin boots from Thierry Mugler, circa 1985. Mugler's exaggerated image of femininity led to many overtly sexual shoe and boot shapes appearing in his catwalk shows.

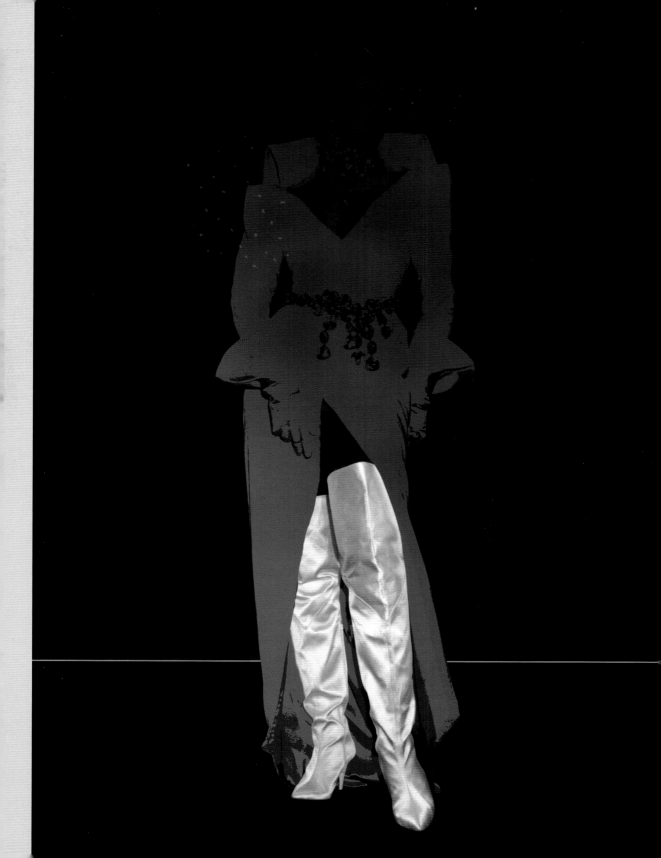

LEFT FROM TOP A selection of 1980s slingbacks: Charles Jourdan white leather strappy slingback from 1980; gold-studded black slingback with gold leather, by Charles Jourdan for Esperento, 1988; white and multicoloured upper with cut-outs from Charles Jourdan, 1983; bronze leather peep-toe with moulded plastic perforated heels from Séducta, 1989.

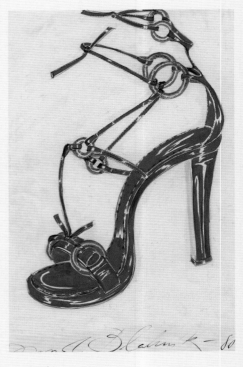

BELOW Manolo Blahnik orange suede pixie boots, circa 1985. Flat-heeled suede ankle boots were a popular unisex style derived from the New Romantic movement.

ABOVE The Ring sandal by Manolo Blahnik, 1984..

OPPOSITE The Perry, named after American fashion designer Perry Ellis, by Manolo Blahnik, 1981.

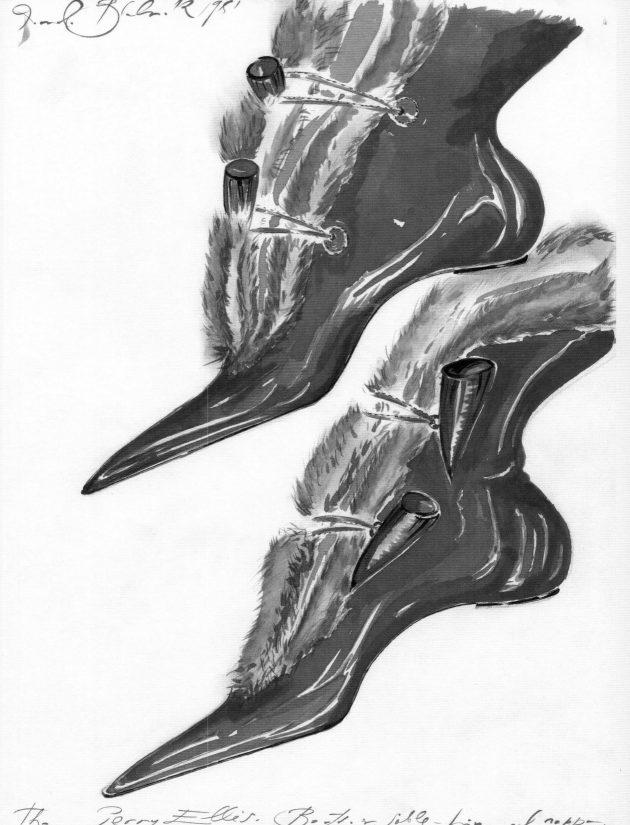

Key Shoe Designers

Maud Frizon (1941–)

Frizon's work was among some of the most exciting of the decade. Born Nadine Frizon in Paris, Frizon began her career in the 1960s as a model for fashion designers Nina Ricci, Jean Patou and the more radical André Courrèges. Most of the time, models were expected to turn up with their hair done and their make-up in place, as this was before the advent of the session stylist. Frizon also found that, whether at a catwalk show or a photo-shoot, she regularly had to come equipped with shoes to complement the designer gear or make a choice from the several pairs available. Usually, the shoes she was forced to wear were so dull that she took the matter into her own hands and started creating her own. By 1969, Frizon had become so adept at creating fantastic handmade footwear that she opened her own boutique in St-Germain-des-Prés, Paris, and came up with the cone heel, which was used in the catwalk collections she produced for Thierry Mugler and Azzedine Alaïa.

By the 1980s, Frizon was at the height of her success with her bold, audacious and very sexy designs that combined exotic skins such as lizard and crocodile with bright suede and dyed canvas. High-heeled pumps with red and black polka dots vied for attention with her black leather cone heels with a white ruffle nail-headed to the back, or a pair of pale almond-green suede gladiator sandals. Peep toes were a speciality as Frizon regarded them as the feet's equivalent of a plunging neckline and, for her, equally as erotic.

Andrea Pfister (1942–)

Another key name in the 1980s was Andrea Pfister, an Italian footwear designer working in Paris. After studying art and languages at the University of Florence in the early 1960s, Pfister switched to the Institute of Footwear Design in Milan and, having found his metier, went on to design shoe collections for Patou and Lanvin, showing the first collection under his own label in 1965. In 1967, Pfister met his partner, Jean-Pierre Dupré, and they opened the first Pfister boutique on the rue Cambon in Paris, a successful business that was consolidated even further when the pair bought a factory that had the capacity to produce 200 pairs of shoes per day.

In Pfister's work, one can see the legacy of André Perugia and his surrealist experiments of the 1930s, and like that other consummate Italian shoe designer, he combines wit with superb craftsmanship. For, as Pfister puts it, 'If a beautiful woman's feet hurt, she becomes ugly.' Throughout the 1980s, his shoes had distinct themes that were summed up in their capricious titles: the Martini Dry, for instance, had a heel in the shape of a cocktail glass with a slice of lemon sticking out of the side, while the Medici was a kidskin pump covered in intricate gold decoration inspired by Florentine book binding.

Pfister's use of clashing colours perfectly fitted in with the strident feel of 1980s fashion, and he experimented with shades that had never been seen before in shoe design as a result of his close collaboration with two important Italian tanneries: the Anaconda, which specialized in reptile skins, and the Stefania, who were experts in leather and suede. Many of his designs combined leather and suede in contrasting colours – such as the whimsical North Pole collection of 1984, which featured black-and-white snakeskin penguins on a green suede ankle boot. The Mosaique shoe was one of the most copied shoes of the 1980s – instantly recognized by its multicoloured patches of snakeskin appliquéd onto a white leather background – while the Tomato mule had a vibrant vegetable-print lining and a red tomato complete with a vine leaf for the heel. In 1984, Pfister's beach sandal was surrealism incarnate, with a lush gold leather lining that had bright red-painted toe-nails to indicate where the feet should sit, and a thong strap which took the form of a striped beach umbrella that arched over the foot to act as a shade from the sun. As Pfister himself put it, 'It's impossible not to smile when you wear a pair of my shoes.'

ABOVE Soft purple leather pumps by Maud Frizon, with uppers in gold leather and with purple mesh-fabric detailing at the toe, quarters and heel. The combination of a softly pointed toe shape and a breasted heel was popular in the mid 1980s.

BELOW Alligator leather pumps with a pointed toe and 9-cm (3.5-inch) stiletto heel by Andrea Pfister, circa 1985.

Walter Steiger (1942–)

Steiger was born in 1942 in Geneva, Switzerland, and
by 1958, he had become an apprentice at Molinard
Bottier in Zurich, where he learned how to make shoes
by hand. In the 1960s, he worked with many of the
key designers associated with the 'Swinging Sixties',
including Mary Quant, and designed shoes for the
seminal movie of the decade, Michelangelo Antonioni's
Blow-Up (1966), while working in the Bally Studio in
the King's Road, London. In 1967, he showed the first
collection under his own name in Paris, and opened
the first Steiger boutique in 1974. By the 1980s, the
designer was collaborating with all the major names
of fashion, including Claude Montana, famed for
his inverted triangle silhouettes with huge padded
shoulders, Karl Lagerfeld, Kenzo and Azzedine Alaïa,
and in America, Bill Blass, Calvin Klein and Oscar de la
Renta. Steiger's shoes summed up the decade – they
were high, sexy and flashy with lots of design detail
such as neon-pink bows or polka dots combined with
black patent, all beautifully handmade in Italy and every
pair completed with a full leather lining. Steiger's 1980s
designs included pewter metallic stilettos with python-
covered heels, ostrich ankle boots, beige snakeskin
slingbacks with hot-pink grosgrain bows, and a new
version of the comma heel that was launched in 1985.

The Intellectual Shoe

Flashy power dressing was one look among many in this eclectic and individualist decade. Money was being spent on appearance and many new young designers began to make their way to the forefront of fashion with a set of radical and experimental ideas. Leading the pack in the first half of the decade were a pair of designers from Japan who caused experienced fashion journalists to drop their Mont Blanc pens in amazement when they first showed in Paris in 1982. Philosophy graduate Rei Kawakubo of Commes des Garçons and Yohji Yamamoto ignored the fashion for status dressing and presented formless black garments on blank-faced models to the sound of discordant music, all illuminated by stark bright lights. *Time* magazine realized their significance and, in 1983, wrote, 'these are not international celebrity couturiers, doing cunning variations on conventional forms. These are revolutionaries, insurgents whose aim is to modify, sometimes even change, the shape and form of clothing itself.'

Kawakubo's Wrapped collection followed her personal philosophy of 'getting down to the essence of shapelessness, formlessness and colourlessness' and consisted of a series of unidentifiable tubular-shaped garments with several sleeves that, when not worn in the traditional way, could be wrapped and tied about the body. Such intellectual fashion needed a serious shoe and the flat black pump based on the traditional footwear of Japanese peasants provided a clear alternative to the glitzy *Dynasty* look.

The designer who made some of the most inventive flat shoes of the decade was Tokio Kumagai (1948–87), born in Sendai, Japan, just after the Second World War. In his tragically short-lived career he was universally celebrated for his elegant, witty footwear that combined functionality with a subversively surrealist streak. In 1970, after graduating from Bunka Fukuso Gakuin, one of Japan's premier fashion colleges, he moved to Paris. There he collaborated with fashion designer Jean-Charles de Castelbajac, who was famed for his outlandish pop art designs such as an anti-fur coat constructed from toy teddy bears, and outsize sweatshirts adorned with a Betty Boop cartoon.

In 1981, Kumagai opened his first boutique in Paris, in the Place des Victoires, and began a trans-global lifestyle, spending eight months in the French capital followed by four months in his native Tokyo. His work embraced both cities too, managing to combine Gallic chic with a Japanese quirkiness, with shoes that masqueraded as cartoon chickens or tiny mice complete with tails that grew out of the back of the shoes, all handmade by Heresco, a shoe-making company in Italy. Kumagai's Rooster shoe, created in 1983, took the form of a simple slip-on white leather

shoe with a low-stacked heel and a vamp decorated with the head of a cockerel, with a coxcomb of red leather, a black leather beak and a black button for the eye. The quarter (the area at the sides and back of the shoe) was cleverly cut and stitched to take the form of the cockerel's wing. Other designs included the Sports Car – a slip-on shoe from 1984 with a square toe and low-stacked heel in navy leather with white leather headlights, grille and wheels and a clear plastic windscreen embedded into the tab – and a flat purple suede pump with the front vamp sculpted to resemble a bunch of grapes, which Kumagai designed just before his death in 1987. His most bizarre designs were the Shoes to Eat series in 1984 that took inspiration from the artificial food used to tempt customers in the windows of downtown Tokyo restaurants. A pair of high heels were covered in strips of red, raw artificial 'beef' made out of acrylic; flat pumps metamorphosed into mounds of red beans and rice; and white stilettos took the form of ice-cream sundaes.

Flat shoes were being played with in London too, as Patrick Cox showed platypus-toed Dolly shoes adorned with oversize chrome buckles to mimic the look of a doll's shoe and flat Minnie Mouse sandals in black leather with a huge cartoon bow at the ankle. His backless ghillies for the fashion designer John Flett mixed up the ballet flat, the mule and the canvas sneaker to create a strange post-modernist hybrid of all three classic designs.

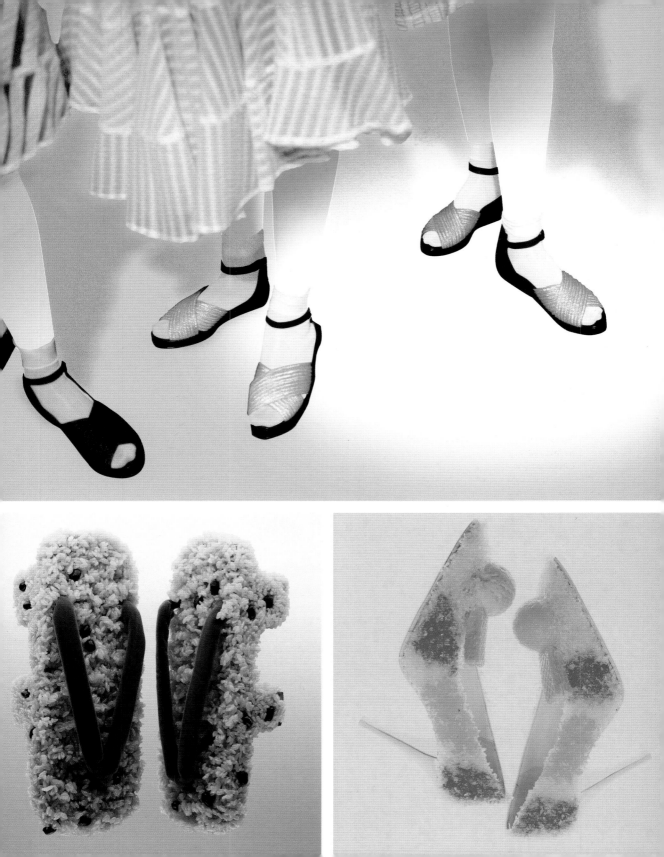

LEFT Vivienne Westwood designs from 1989; black patent leather buckled stilettos are on the left and black patent cut-out boots with straps and buckles appear right.

BELOW Fetishist Charles Jourdan black satin shoes circa 1985 with black metal-studded elastic anklecuff showing the continuing influence of 1970s punk.

The Subversive Shoe

In the middle years of the decade, street style met catwalk chic in the work of young designers Jean-Paul Gaultier, Stephen Sprouse, and David Holah and Stevie Stewart – the latter two worked under the name of Bodymap. Their take on fashion was much more playful, anarchic and fun and was related less to the harsh world of work and far more to underground movements such as hip hop or New Romanticism, a style with a theatrical form of cross-dressing that was taking over in European clubs and pop culture in the form of the groups Adam and the Ants, Duran Duran and Spandau Ballet. This counter-cultural look was totally different from mainstream fashion and operated on a principle of blurring the differences between male and female. Young males wore make-up, frilled shirts and pixie boots quite openly and were applauded for their experimentation, with singer-songwriter Boy George becoming a national treasure. Singers Annie Lennox and Grace Jones cropped their hair and wore men's suits – fashion's boundaries were being crossed and there was no such thing as strictly gendered dress.

New Romantic dressing was about being individual and creative rather than being decked out from head to toe in the latest designer gear, and history was used as source material that could be jumbled up and re-assembled at will. The work of Vivienne Westwood in the early 1980s exemplifies this cut-and-paste approach, as she took inspiration from eighteenth-century pirates, Peruvian culture and New York graffiti and mixed it up with her inspirational and anarchic punk aesthetic.

Westwood's shoe shapes in the 1980s went wilfully against the grain of footwear fashion as she ignored both stiletto heels and serious flats in her catwalk shows. In the historical and romantic Pirate Collection of 1981 Westwood threw off the vestiges of punk:

shirts had ruffled fronts, trousers were eighteenth century in design, trainer toes were squared off into a 'hammerhead' shape and Westwood presented her first version of the definitive multi-buckled low stack-heeled pirate boot, which continues to be sold today. In the 1982 Buffalo collection, models square-danced down the catwalk to Appalachian folk music wearing mud as make-up and deliberately bulky clothes that were 'paddicoated' under dropwaisted skirts and worn with raw wool drawstring trousers, huge hats and duck-billed shoes. Blancmange-pink satin bras were worn as outerwear and huge felt hats were accessorized with sack and bag boots, which totally obscured the foot and were literally leather bags or sacks with soles and stacked Cuban or Louis heels – they made the stiletto heel look matronly and staid by comparison. Westwood's Witches collection of 1983 saw the introduction of the three-tongued white leather platform trainer, which had a trio of outsized tongues that flopped lasciviously over the front and had oval eyelets for the laces outlined in chrome.

New shoe shapes were devised that were both physically and intellectually demanding to wear but also fun. In her typically subversive way, Westwood, with a nudge from Patrick Cox in 1984, devised a new form of the platform that was first seen in Cox's designs for the Clint Eastwood collection in shoes that were raised 7.5 cm (3 inches) off the ground at the front and 11.5 cm (4½ inches) at the back. Westwood then devised her own unique version, the Rocking Horse wedge, which was applied to boots, shoes and slave sandals. The name derived from the rocking motion the wearer had to make backwards and forwards in order to negotiate walking safely in them, as the wooden platforms had absolutely no flexibility. Westwood wore them while riding her bike, resplendent in a polka-dot mini crinoline stiffened with wire and a Harris tweed crown. The block-soled Rocking Horse designs made conscious reference to the ancient Venetian chopine shoe and, quite literally, put women on a pedestal, while Westwood's other styles with obvious shock value would later include the Penis shoe of 1995.

BELOW LEFT Vivienne Westwood's Savage collection from 1982 featured shoes and boots in this archaic sacklike shape.

BELOW CENTRE Westwood's Rocking Horse golf shoes in brown leather. Throughout the 1980s and into the 1990s Westwood continued to experiment with extreme shapes. To show the functionality of her Rocking Horse shoes Westwood used to wear a pair to cycle to work.

BELOW RIGHT Westwood's iconic multi-strapped pirate boots from the early 1980s with her iconic squiggle-print design. The Pirate boot is still in production today.

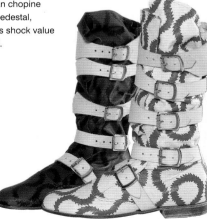

Body-conscious Dressing

The 1980s vogue for experimental dressing meant that other, less anarchic catwalk looks by European fashion designers were copied and subverted by young women and worn in ways their creators hadn't intended. The trend for body-conscious dressing is a case in point, associated with two designers, Hervé Léger and Azzedine Alaïa. Léger's spandex stretch-bandage minis in jewel-bright colours exaggerated the female form into an hourglass shape while keeping the body under corseted control. Tunisian-born designer Alaïa, dubbed the 'King of Cling' by the fashion press, energized high-street fashion in the mid to late 1980s with his trademark black jersey contoured mini-dresses, leggings and cropped leather jackets. Alaïa's designs were body conscious and renowned for the way they displayed the female form, and perfectly caught the mood of the times, as many women had turned to exercise to hone their bodies into toned and muscled sculptures. Alaïa's tailoring was complex and some dresses had up to 40 separate pieces that acted as a web of corsetry, hugging the body in all the right places in the form of a second skin. His skintight and stretchy designs covered the bodies of off-duty top models such as Naomi Campbell and Eva Herzigova, and stars such as Tina Turner and Brigitte Nielsen, who wore them with high heels to create a hyper-sexual image.

This high-glamour look changed dramatically when it reached the high street and French seduction was combined with avant-garde elements from Kawakubo, Yamamoto and Vivienne Westwood. Alaïa's killer heels were replaced with clumpy boots, changing the look from glamorous vamp to street-smart urchin, and by doing so playfully rejected the traditional notion that for a woman to be feminine she had to have tiny feet. For the first time in history, the dimensions of women's feet were deliberately exaggerated by heavy-soled shoes or work boots, which, when combined with a thigh-high body-contoured mini and opaque black tights, owed much to Popeye's cartoon love interest, Olive Oyl.

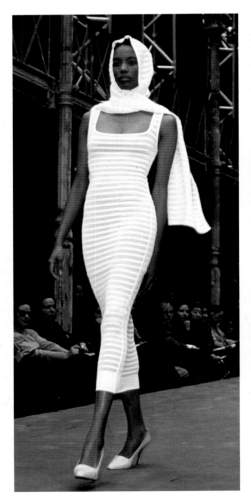

Brothel-creepers and Boots

This new vibe meant that a utilitarian classic, the steel-toed DM or Dr Marten boot, enjoyed a wave of popularity. The standard-issue black leather lace-up boot was the complete antithesis of the corporate Yuppie look; its natural habitat was the factory floor, not the executive boardroom, and it was traditionally worn by workers as a form of protective footwear. Recognizing that DM's were the perfect anti-fashion fashion statement, Kawakubo, Yamamoto and Bodymap used DM boots in their catwalk presentations, but the designers who made the look tip over into the mainstream were Wayne and Geraldine Hemingway, also known as Red or Dead, who set up their label in 1982, and Patrick Cox, who deconstructed the traditional Dr Marten boot in 1984.

Cox was a student studying footwear design at Cordwainer's College in London when, on his way there one morning, he saw a construction worker kicking debris off his feet by banging the end of his steel-capped boot against a brick wall. This heavy treatment had left the steel cap bursting through the leather of the shoe. Cox traced the brand, found they were classic Dr Martens and customized the boot by stripping away the leather, exposing the steel toe and polishing it. This revised classic caught the mood for sturdy shoes and 80 pairs of these industrial-looking boots were sold in Bazaar in South Molton Street every week.

The Hemingway empire commenced in Camden Market, London, where the couple set up a series of lucrative market stalls that sold an eclectic mixture of Geraldine's fashion designs, vintage clothes and original Dr Marten boots. Hemingway saw that the rise of the DM boot was all about timing, 'There were all these girls wearing tight black dresses, and we changed the silhouette by putting a bloody big pair of boots at the end. Then everyone wanted them – Jean-Paul Gaultier was buying them from our stall in Camden, Demi Moore, and every star you could think of, it was unbelievable.'

The plain black boot was a perfect black canvas that could be customized by the owner to give a semblance of individuality, and the first market stall customers did just that by adding coloured laces and paint effects. Wayne and Geraldine followed suit with their own versions and then approached the company and began working in tandem with them to produce a range in wild colours, ultra-shiny patent finishes and exposed metal toe caps; their most eccentric design was in 1990 when a pair of transparent Doc Marten boots was shown as part of their Space Baby collection.

By 1984, the couple began to design their own shoes, many featuring the thick roller sole that anticipated the revival of the platform in the early 1990s. Toe shapes were ultra-round and when

combined with rubber bumper platforms gave them the look of dodgem cars, a fun element that was reinforced when the Union Jack was painted or appliquéd on the vamps. Their elevated silhouette had become mainstream by the 1990s thanks to the antics of the British pop group the Spice Girls and the spread of so-called 'Girl Power'. Buffalo trainers with thick rubber-tread soles situated the look firmly in teenage culture rather than post-punk fashion, and its youthful exuberance meant new footwear styles were sought by women wanting a return to a more classic kind of chic.

BELOW The crepe-soled brothel creeper was revived from 1950s menswear and worn by both sexes in the 1980s as a subversive take on androgynous dressing. Here it accompanies the post-modern play of Jean-Paul Gaultier's 1987 collection.

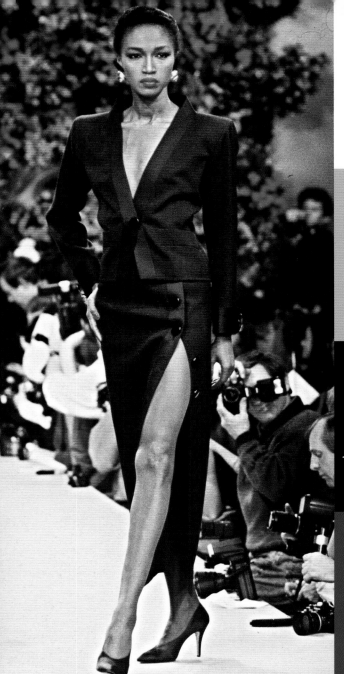

◄ **Cone heels**

The cone heel was a key shape, use[d] by many of the top footwear designe[rs] such as Blahnik, Pfister and Frizon. A[ ] modern take on the high heel, it was easier to walk in than the stiletto and serious yet sexy shape that could be worn in the office and the nightclub. This evening sandal with rosette is b[y] Charles Jourdan, a label that was on[e] of the most popular in the 1980s.

Key looks of the decade

1980s

▲ **Stiletto spike heels**

The spike heel enjoyed a tremendous revival as fashion became more spectacular. The padded shoulders of the power suit could appear a little masculine if accompanied with flats. When a pair of high stiletto heels were worn, the look was Amazonian, a mix of metropolitan chic meets dominatrix. This evening ensemble by Yves Saint Laurent exemplifies the look in 1989.

▲ **Boots**

The revival of the mini meant that boots came right back into fashion and enjoyed the same popularity as the 1960s. The length of leg expose[d] by the short skirt could be encased [in] black polished leather, as in this pair by Katherine Hamnett dating from 1988. Ankle, knee and thigh boots were all seen on the streets by the end of the decade.

Toe decoration

[Th]e lifestyle of the young professional [wa]s all about conspicuous [co]nsumption – if you've got money, [flau]nt it! Both day and evening shoes [had] a lot of embellishment and the [gen]tly rounded toe became both a [foc]al point and blank canvas on which [to] display various kinds of pattern-[ma]king and intricate techniques, as [se]en in these mid-1980s Gina shoes.

▾ Loafers
Between home and office many women took off their heels and walked in trainers and the more upmarket equivalent, the loafer. Tods were one of the most exclusive brands and remain successful today. Their classic loafer or driving shoe is instantly recognizable because of the grippers on the extended sole.

▲ Dr Marten boots
This functional boot has been associated with street rebellion since it was adopted by skinheads in the 1970s. In the 1980s it became a subversive style worn by women who wanted to diffuse the overt sexuality of body-conscious dressing and give a fresh youthful look to the silhouette. Dr Martens appeared in the catwalk shows of radical designers such as Body Map and Yohji Yamamoto.

[A]nkle boot
[The] ankle boot could be sky-high [and] overtly sexy, as in this snakeskin [stile]tto-heeled example by Terry De [Hav]illand, or totally flat and unisex with [the] suede Tukka. As black leggings [gre]w in popularity so did the ankle [boo]t, the perfect footwear to act as a [foc]al point.

▸ Wedge heels and commas
Past styles were rediscovered, revitalized and revived. The stiletto was followed by the cone, the wedge and the comma. Revivals of experimental heel shapes can be recognized by their exaggeration and overt sexiness with the use of bright colours, extreme decoration and high-patent shine. Here Thierry Mugler played with the wedge in 1986.

1990s to Now:

Future Collectables

At the beginning of the 1990s, the Dr Marten boot was still the footwear of choice among rebellious teenage 'Riot Girls' and fans of Seattle grunge music, and a scuffed pair were worn by Courtney Love, the wife of Nirvana's Kurt Cobain, with bias-cut 1930s tea dresses, ripped fishnet stockings and a slash of red lipstick. A change was coming, though, and it took the form of an unprecedented interest in shoes as many women were prepared to spend more money than ever before on accessories.

The stiletto heel underwent a tremendous change in fortune and became the most popular shoe style in the 1990s and early 2000s, holding its own at the top for over 15 years. The American television series *Sex and the City* helped by making a causal relationship between success, killer heels and a successful sexual life as the key character Carrie, played by Sarah Jessica Parker, began to be photographed wearing designer shoes, usually by Jimmy Choo or Manolo Blahnik, both on and off the studio set. In fact, Blahnik's heels continued to be coveted by celebrities and civilians alike. Kylie Minogue chose to wear white leather stiletto-heeled winklepickers by Blahnik for her crucial comeback album 'Fever' in 2001, and Madonna pronounced his shoes 'as good as sex. And they last longer'.

Flashbulbs also popped in 1993 when supermodel Naomi Campbell tripped up and sprawled at the end of the catwalk in a pair of 25-cm (10-inch) high super-elevated court shoes by Vivienne Westwood, an exaggerated platform-heel design that had first made an appearance in her 1990s Portrait collection. These notorious shoes now have pride of place in the Victoria and Albert Museum and are one of their most popular exhibits. It took commitment to wear Westwood's shoes and many women were prepared to follow the 'no pain no gain' ethos, particularly if the pair that was pinching their toes came in the shape of Tom Ford's deadly spike metal heels for Gucci, dubbed 'push-up bras' for the feet. And, rather alarmingly, many women agreed with Sarah Jessica Parker when she said, 'I could run a marathon in a pair of Manolo heels. I can race out and hail a cab. I can run up Sixth Avenue at full speed. I've destroyed my feet completely, but I don't care. What do you really need your feet for anyway?'

Today's Designers, Tomorrow's Collectables

In the last two decades, the names of shoe designers have become public knowledge and entered everyday vocabulary as fashion has become increasingly fashionable. At the moment, the market is dominated by major brands and the odds are stacked against new, young designers who produce their ranges in small quantities and find it hard to get a foothold in any major retail space. Many established department stores are resistant to new, untested labels, so the route nowadays is to collaborate with a fashion designer on a catwalk show – the downside of which is that the shoes are secondary to the clothes and the footwear designer's name is sometimes a tad invisible. Names to look out for in the future are Adele Clarke, who has worked with Hussein Chalayan; Olivia Morris, known for her flesh-coloured leather tattoo boots that are covered with hearts and daggers and who has collaborated with Matthew Williamson; and Nicholas Kirkwood, whose towering platforms and vertiginous heels have appeared on the runway of several Chloé shows. Two outstanding creatives in the field of footwear today are Benoît Méléard, the only shoe designer to present a runway show during Paris Fashion Week and whose 'cruel' shoes, as he dubs them, with circular toes and invisible heels, assume the most fantastic shapes, and the sublime Pierre Hardy, whose work for Nicolas Ghesquière at Balenciaga is never off the fashion radar.

Some names remain the same. Gina continues to make bejewelled evening sandals, carrying on a tradition of hand-craftsmanship that has existed in the family firm since the 1950s, and 'rock 'n' roll' cobbler Terry de Havilland still engineers ingenious platforms out of patchwork python in his own inimitable way, just around the corner in the East End of London. Other names have joined them to become major players on the contemporary footwear scene, including the global brands of Jimmy Choo, Sergio Rossi and Cesare Paciotti, woman designers Emma Hope and Georgina Goodman, and the genius that is Christian Louboutin, a designer who truly understands the psychological as well as physiological meanings of shoes. Shoes have become sites of extreme artistic experimentation – Pierre Hardy's futuristic techno-industrial aesthetic, which features metal mesh and cogged chains attached to geometric uppers and heavy conical heels, is a welcome change from the legions of glitzy sandals that have dominated the market. His eclectic inspirations range from the Italian post-modernist designer Ettore Sottsass in the 1980s to post-war American Abstract Expressionism. Footwear production has changed markedly too, with large-scale manufacturing being farmed out to countries such as India, Vietnam, Indonesia and China – and many worry that quality is being sacrificed on the altar of economics.

OVERLEAF Supermodel Christy Turlington wears a pair of platform-heel gold satin ankle-strap Gina shoes in the 1990s.

RIGHT TOP Vivienne Westwood's On Liberty collection from 1994 featuring a Cromwellian square toe shape.

RIGHT Westwood's Cuban-heeled ankle boot from her Vive la Cocotte collection in 1995; overtly sexy with a nod to glam rock.

BELOW RIGHT Terry de Havilland's Poppy, first designed in 2006 and famously worn by singer Amy Winehouse. Its Pop Art styling is in homage to the work of Roy Lichtenstein.

BOTTOM RIGHT The original Margaux by Terry de Havilland was designed in 1975 but has remained incredibly popular; this is a modern version seen on the feet of Kate Moss and Sienna Miller.

BELOW A selection of shoes from up-and-coming designer Nicolas Kirkwood's 2008 collection, which show the extreme height of the heel that is popular in high fashion.

LEFT Vivienne Westwood shoes are always adventurous and unexpected. Here a pair of shoes are accompanied by huge bright orange leather gaiters cum legwarmers in 2007.

RIGHT AND BELOW 'Space-age' styles in 1995 from Gina. Right is the Odyssey boot, created from layering three materials, and below is the Christie, a white suede upper with a fine steel gauze over a translucent heel.

ABOVE A Marilyn Monroe-inspired mule from Gina in 2000. A red mesh upper has a crocodile-embossed patent bow decorated with Swarovski crystals.

THIS PAGE A selection of Swarovski-studded Gina shoes from recent collections, including the 2002 Tatianna thong sandal, top left; the iconic and much-copied 2003 Zeta mule, above right; a red satin belted boot with buckle from 2000, left; and different versions of the Cinderella-like slipper, Gilda, from 2005, below.

ABOVE A crocodile-embossed velvet boot from Gina, 1999, with a chainmail Swarovski cuff and heel.

Jimmy Choo (1948–)

Born in 1948 in Penang, Malaysia, into a family of shoemakers, Jimmy Choo came to London to study at Cordwainers College in 1985. In 1986, he opened his workshop in the East End and began creating exclusive handmade shoes, which three years later were given an unprecedented eight-page feature in British *Vogue*. Jimmy Choo was the footwear label of choice for Princess Diana, who would buy one style in several different colours, and *Vogue* accessories editor Tamara Mellon. All of Choo's shoes were entirely handmade on the premises and his increasing fame meant that the supply could not keep up with the demand – he was handmaking two pairs per day. Mellon, sensing a business opportunity and realizing there was a gap in the market for a competitor to Manolo Blahnik, bought into the business. With an investment stake of £150,000, Mellon started the ready-to-wear branch of the label with the shoes being made in Italy.

In 2001, the company split with Jimmy Choo, who was bought out of his 50 per cent stake by Robert Bensoussan in order to concentrate on exclusive handmade designs at Jimmy Choo Couture, which operates out of Connaught Street, London. Choo's wife's niece, Sandra Choi, who trained under him, became Design Director with Mellon in charge of business strategy for the ready-to-wear line. By 2004, the company had opened an unprecedented 26 new stores and diversified into handbags. That same year, the company was valued at £100 million and is now the best-known name in luxury shoes.

The success of the label is more to do with the brand image projected by the jet-set lifestyle of Tamara Mellon and the celebrities who wear the shoes on the red carpet rather than cutting-edge design – although the shoes are fashion-lead and very beautiful due to Mellon's knowledge of style through her stint at *Vogue*. The company's annual tie-in with the Academy Awards (or Oscars) ceremony in Hollywood was a clever move – in the week prior to the glitzy show, Choo sets up shop at the Peninsula Hotel or Raffles L'Ermitage Hotel, Beverley Hills, to make their shoes available to the stars, with many of the shoes hand-dyed and beaded to be an exact match with the colour of the dramatic gowns. Consequently, many of the female Oscar winners such as Hilary Swank, Halle Berry and Julia Roberts have accepted their statuettes wearing a pair of Jimmy Choos in images that are beamed across the world. In 2003, Sandra Choi explained the Choo look: 'The Choo heel is not a killer heel. When women think Jimmy Choo they think diamanté, evening, sexy. The shoes are accessible. It's not an intimidating brand.'

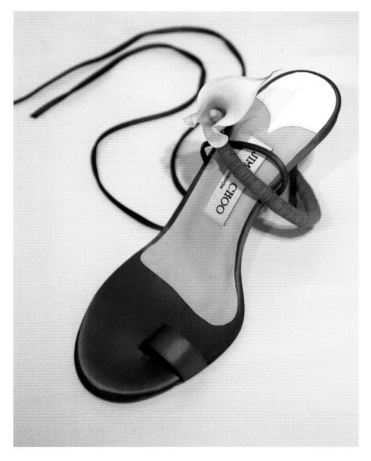

OPPOSITE Manolo Blahnik continues to make iconic collectable shoes, including the multicoloured Aksham shoe, opposite top, and the gold Kucuk, opposite bottom. Here the design drawings are transformed into beautifully examples of shoe ergonomics.

ABOVE Sublime simplicity in this delicate thong sandal from Jimmy Choo, 2003.

Sergio Rossi (1935–)

Rossi's establishment of a global shoe brand is a classic rags to riches story. Born in the small town of San Mauro Pascali, Italy, in 1935, Rossi was the son of a traditional shoemaker from whom he learnt the trade. At the age of 14, he was forced to take over the business when his father died. From this inauspicious beginning, Rossi and his brother Franco created a leading Italian shoe brand that encapsulates the glamour of la dolce vita in the same way as the fashion designs of Dolce & Gabbana and Donatella Versace.

In the 1950s, the brothers travelled to Milan at a time when the city was being presented as a centre of fashion fit to rival Paris and Ferragamo was transforming the image of the Italian footwear industry. Rossi's artisan skills were supplemented with training in aesthetics and design development, and he began selling shoes to shops in Bologna and sandals on the beach at Rimini. One particular style, the Opanca, a sandal with red leather straps and a wooden sole that curled up to hold the feet at the sides, caught the eye of a journalist who introduced Rossi to a German manufacturer, who promised to set up an Italian factory to mass-produce Rossi's work. Although the backer ultimately pulled out, the factory opened in 1966 and, despite an initial mountain of debt, the brothers began to succeed, helped by the fact that partisan fashion designers in Milan were happy to collaborate with home-grown shoe designers.

By the 1980s, the Rossi brothers were working with the most exciting designers to have come out of Italy since Emilio Pucci, including Dolce & Gabbana and Gianni Versace. The first Rossi boutique opened in 1980 and was followed by a period of rapid expansion; stores in Turin, Rome, New York, Los Angeles and London soon followed as women bought into the sexy brand image that was being created by an instantly recognizable advertising campaign in the 1990s, which was inspired by the work of fashion photographer Helmut Newton. Models such as Naomi Campbell and Carla Bruni, who was something of a muse, were shown as powerful and sexually dominant, shot from the feet upwards to give a fetishist emphasis to the high heel – which is always at least 7.5 cm (3 inches) high.

Rossi's shoes and black patent boots are masterpieces of Italian modernism. They consist of simple shapes and pure lines in one clear colour and are designed to lengthen the leg rather than break it up with extraneous decoration – in an era of extravagant overdesign, this makes for a refreshing change. In 1990, the company was bought by the Gucci Group, and in 2006 Puerto Rican shoe meister Edmund Castillo took over as design director.

LEFT A luxurious Russian-inspired Sergio Rossi fur-cuffed cream suede boot from 2005.

OPPOSITE Gold leather ankle-tie stiletto evening sandal by Sergio Rossi, a modern evocation of the 1920s tango shoe reinterpreted for 2004.

BELOW A scalloped-quarter gold leather evening shoe from Sergio Rossi, 2004.

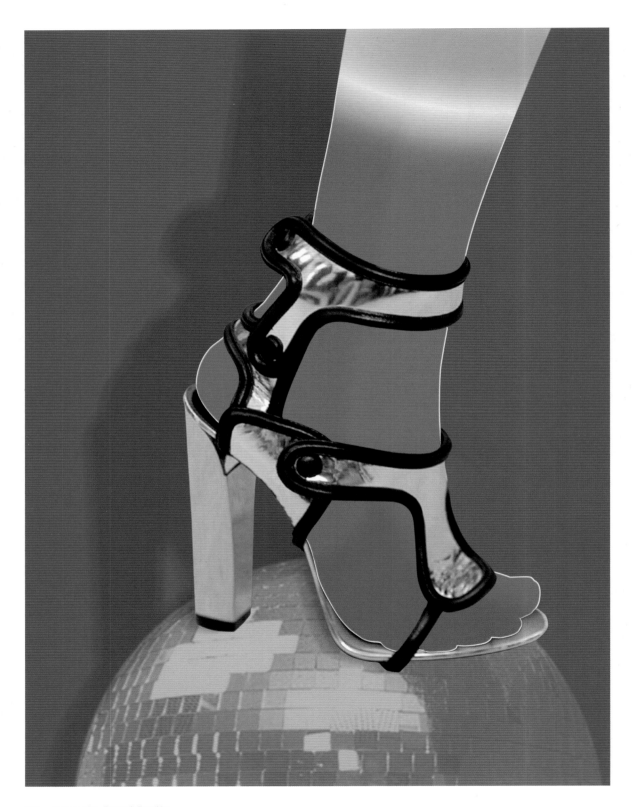

OPPOSITE AND ABOVE The designer shoe is coveted in the 2000s and the female consumer has to get on a waiting list for the season's must-have. Opposite is a Balenciaga design from 2006 and above is a high-gloss high-fashion stiletto by Gucci from 2003.

RIGHT FROM TOP Gladiator-style platform sandals for Gucci 2006 by designer Stuart Weitzman; a high-octane pair of black corded silk sandals with a high rod heel pierced by a diamanté ball by Stuart Weitzman for Gucci 2004–5; women's black patent T-bars with a high heel covered in patent leather and laced chain by Versace, 2005

Christian Louboutin (1963–)

Christian Louboutin's obsession with shoes dates from an early age; in fact, he remembers in 1973, around the age of ten, strolling past the Museum of Oceanography in Paris and being stopped short by a sign warning women not to enter if they were wearing stilettos – the sign must have been a relic from the 1950s. At that moment, he realized two things: that shoes could be transgressive, even dangerous objects and that in an age when platforms and wedges dominated fashion, there were other alternatives which could be retrieved from the dustbin of history. As he put it:

'I could not believe that someone could design something so curious and I realized that I could draw something that did not exist. I realized you could do what you want with a drawing of a shoe. Little by little I collected information and people began to bring anything about shoes to school for me. Someone gave me a gold book, nothing on the cover, just the name 'Roger Vivier' and I saw these incredible shoes… My God! It can really be a job!'

At 17, Louboutin was partying in Left Bank nightclubs and hanging out backstage at the fabled Folies Bergère. He was transfixed by the glamour and hypnotic sexual power of the showgirls and the magnificent way they could manoeuvre in staggeringly high heels without looking down at their feet to spoil the illusion. He became an apprentice with Charles Jourdan in Romans, near Lyon, in 1981, and then freelanced for Maud Frizon and Yves Saint Laurent, with whom he had a long collaboration. To Louboutin's great honour, Saint Laurent allowed Louboutin's name to be paired with his on the label – this was the first

time in Saint Laurent's career that he had allowed this to happen, echoing the relationship between Christian Dior and Roger Vivier. In fact, Louboutin went on to work with Vivier in 1988 when he was asked to help put together a retrospective exhibition of the designer's work, despite being 40 years his junior. Here he was introduced to Vivier's most iconic and experimental designs, including the diamanté ball-heeled pumps designed for Marlene Dietrich that had a lasting influence on the young shoemaker.

In 1992, Christian Louboutin opened his flagship boutique in Paris, where he continues to showcase some of the world's most avant-garde, openly erotic and occasionally simply quirky shoes. The Love shoe, for instance, was an early design inspired by a press photograph of Princess Diana looking melancholy while staring down at her feet at an official function that appeared to be boring her. Louboutin had the idea of creating a pair of shoes that would have made her smile instead, and made a pair that when placed next to one another simply spelt out the word 'Love'. Another early design, the Trash mule, with a saucy shape inspired by his beloved showgirls, had a Perspex heel that contained old Metro tickets and other bits of recycled rubbish found on the streets of Paris. His more recent designs still retain a tinge of surrealism – the black suede slingbacked Kobe shoe of 2004 has a man's tie hanging down over the front, and the Rodita zip platform of 2008 has a zip that endlessly curls around the foot yet has no practical function.

Louboutin shoes stand out from the crowd, not least because of their uncompromisingly sexy, almost fetishist qualities, but also because of their bright red soles. The idea came while the designer was working on a collection that was influenced by the American

Pop artist Andy Warhol and his use of bright, highly saturated colours. After the initial design drawings were done, Louboutin felt something was missing and noticed that one of the assistants was painting her nails with bright red lacquer. He took the bottle and painted the soles of the shoes with the gloss so that though some of the shoes looked demure on the outside, once a woman was walking they gave a flirtatious flash. This is the only form of advertising Louboutin has ever done – it's subliminal, subversive and sexy, like the shoes themselves, and he goes to great lengths to ensure this trademark is not copied by other designers.

Louboutin's heels, such as for his Very Prive or Bruges styles, are some of the highest in the business, and in the 2000s, go beyond subtle sexual suggestion revealing their weapon-like qualities and rendering many women immobile. But as he puts it, 'The last thing I would like is for people to point to my shoes and say, "Oh, they look so comfortable."' The designer continues, 'Women come into the shop and they complain, they say, "I can't run in these shoes!" I say, "Why run? In the reality of life nobody's running… If you walk in a certain rhythm you can watch the city, see the buildings, you see more of the landscape – and it permits men to stop you."'

The Troulala shoe of 2003 is typical of his peep-toe shoes, a style he finds the most erotic as it shows little of the feet and reveals only what Louboutin calls 'the second décolleté' or cleavage of the toe. In the Troulala design, the entire big toe pokes out rather suggestively, 'just waiting to be kissed', says the designer. This black or fire-engine-red shiny patent stiletto heel

transforms the sartorial language of fetishism into high fashion – and recently, Louboutin's interest in extreme shoes has been taken to artistic heights. In 2007, he collaborated with film director David Lynch, a man known for his powerfully dark and compelling films such as *Blue Velvet* (1986) and *Mulholland Drive* (2001), in an art installation entitled 'Fetish', which was held at the Galerie du Passage in Paris. It consisted of a display of five limited-edition pairs of Louboutin shoes shown alongside five signed photographs of the shoes by David Lynch. Louboutin was allowed full creative rein with the shoe designs, and because they had no practical or commercial constraints, his aesthetic was pushed to its limits. Heels were 25-cm (10-inches) high and brought the model's foot into a totally vertical position, like a ballet dancer posing en pointe. Other designs for the exhibition had metal heels that were longer than the body of the shoe and so could only be worn lying down, and a pair of 'Siamese' shoes that were fused together at the heel.

Addiction to shoes is now endemic in our culture – it's one of the few fetishisms that women admit to and legions of fashionistas are prepared to sit on a long waiting list for the right pair of Marc Jacobs, Miu Miu or Prada shoes. Shoes are being bought like never before and prices being paid are higher too, as many women realize that a handmade pair of designer shoes can be a good investment on many levels – they'll last longer, fit more comfortably and look better, and who knows, for the next generation of shoe lovers they could prove to be a very sound investment.

Shopping and Collecting

In the early twenty-first century there has been a new consumer awakening as people have come to their senses and realized that collecting vintage is the most eco-friendly way of buying fashion – it's a perfect example of recycling. The other beauty of collecting vintage is that you can get an item that no-one else has and that's why it's become somewhat of an international pastime. Footwear designers unashamedly pay homage to designs of the past and consequently over the last few years there has been an increasing demand for vintage shoes, as they can sometimes be almost indistinguishable from their modern counterparts. Miu Miu's homage to Terry de Havilland's platform shoes in the early 2000s are an obvious example and had an added bonus – they made the 1970s originals much sought-after and led to a resurrection of the original designer's career. De Havilland's gorgeous pop-art python skin heels now regularly sell for high prices at auction.

Where to Buy

There are obvious outlets for vintage shoes: specialist vintage clothing fairs; retro clothing markets like Portobello Road and Brick Lane in London and the Clignacourt flea-market in Paris; vintage retail outfits such as Exquisite Fashion in New York and Gray's Antique Centre in London; and of course the Internet. Charity and thrift shops are also surprisingly good for vintage shoes, despite having dried up as a source for most other forms of vintage, because the market is still relatively new and untapped and the names of couture shoe designers are far less well known than those associated with clothes. It is still possible to pick up a pair of original stilettos by Salvatore Ferragamo or a pair of 1940s wedges, for instance, because they have been mistaken for the modern version. There are several ways of recognizing a collectable vintage shoe:

- The very best – including Roger Vivier for Christian Dior, Courreges and Beth Levine – will have a *griffe* or designer label inside and these are the ones to collect. The vintage shoes that hold their value are by individual designers rather than mainstream manufacturers. So look for a designer's name like Seymour Troy rather than a corporate name like Dolci's.

- The most expensive designer shoes will be completely made of leather, including a leather lining and will say so: 'all leather' if English, '*cuir*' if French, '*vero cuio*' if Italian.

- Look for leather that is stitched together rather than glued, as again, this suggests a higher quality and hand-made shoe.

- Remember that some synthetic shoes are still collectable, particularly from the 1960s when many of the top designers such as Beth Levine experimented with plastics.

- Original 1950s stilettos will have metal heel tips, not plastic ones.

- Many original manufacturer's labels before the 1960s are written in a calligraphic 'signature' style rather than in modern typography.

To Wear or Not to Wear?

Collectors recognize that many vintage shoes are of a quality that is rarely found today. Techniques like hand-sewn seams and delicate detailing are too expensive to be incorporated into the modern processes of manufacturing footwear. Shoes from the past can also be in quite fragile condition, particularly if they date from the days of cobbling when investing in a pair of shoes was an expensive, long-term purchase and they would have been looked after and worn for many years. So should one wear such fragile objects or, like some collectors, use them to make a decorative statement instead? Many diehard collectors would regard putting on vintage shoes to pound the streets as a sacrilege and instead keep their special finds wrapped in acid-free tissue paper and out of direct sunlight, with a photograph stuck to the front of each box for easy recognition. It must be remembered that many women's shoes from the past were not designed for practicality and nineteenth-century slippers would fall apart if walked for the distances we expect today.

Another reason why vintage shoes remain unworn by many collectors is the question of fit. It is very difficult to find a perfect fit between a vintage shoe and a modern foot because forty years ago feet were considerably smaller – or women pretended they were. Shoes tended to err on the small and narrow side because of the worship of the small and delicate female foot, particularly in the nineteenth and early twentieth century. It is much easier to find larger fitting shoe sizes from the 1970s onwards, as this was the era when the fashion for the clumpy shoe took off; there are bargains to be had from these decades that easily fit in with today's retro-inspired fashions. But if you are determined to collect vintage shoes that fit the following steps should be taken to avoid blisters.

THIS PAGE Gina T-bar peep-toe shoes from the 1960s in white calfskin and navy patent leather.

- Like any shoe, make sure there is enough space at the end to flex your toes. If your foot moves out of the heel when walking, buy an insole for a snug fit.

- If you are buying shoes from eBay or any similar Internet auction site, take no notice of the size that is quoted in the description – shoe sizes from the past vary wildly. Ask the seller for exact width and length measurements and see if they match your feet before purchase. Some sellers also will accept returns so make sure you check their conditions of sale; you may be able to send a pair back if you're not happy with your purchase.

- If the shoes are a little tight, don't despair. It is possible to stretch them a little. For leather, take the shoe and dampen the pinching area with a 50–50 mix of water and methylated spirit or specialist leather lotion and then insert into a shoe stretcher or shoe tree where it should stay until it has dried. If the shoe is synthetic, place it on a shoe stretcher or shoe tree and warm carefully with a hair dryer while pulling it into shape.

- It's very difficult to track down pairs in unworn or very good used condition because shoes, unlike other kinds of retro accessories, were worn, mended and re-mended until they were worn out. As a result, it is fairly unlikely that a collector would find an unused, pristine pair in their original box, but it does happen, especially with 1980s shoes when designer shoes were displayed as trophy items and sometimes hardly worn.

- Finding shoes that date from before the twentieth century is a pretty rare occurrence, but a tip for dating a rare early shoe is to look at the soles. Before the mid-nineteenth century there was no clear distinctions between the left foot or the right; shoes were interchangeable and had identically shaped soles.

Despite recent interest in all things vintage, there are bargains to be had out there. For example, it's much cheaper to buy a pair of Chanel shoes than a blouse or belt, and there is a specific cultural reason for this – people are squeamish about other people's feet. A vintage dress can be easily cleaned, but shoes less so, and many bear the imprint of the previous owner's feet, which can be off-putting to some vintage clothes' enthusiasts. Shoes tend to have a bit more wear and tear than other items of vintage clothing and it's sometimes difficult to disguise. But a suede brush, a shoe shine kit and a pair of insoles can work wonders, and remember that buying vintage is the best way to stand out form the high-street crowd.

Museums and collections

UNITED KINGDOM

Gallery of Costume

Platt Hall,
Rusholme,
Manchester M14 5LL
+44 (0)161 224 5217
www.manchestergalleries.org
One of Britain's largest collections
of clothing, shoes and accessories,
dating from the seventeenth century
to the present day.

Museum of Costume

Bennett Street,
Bath BA1 2QH
+44 (0)1225 477 173
www.museumofcostume.co.uk
Iconic fashion designs, with a collection
including nearly 1300 pairs of shoes
from the 1700s to the present day.

**Northampton Museum
and Art Gallery**

Guildhall Road,
Northampton NN1 1DP
+44 (0)1604 838 111
World famous collection of shoes
and boots, celebrating Northampton's
shoemaking history and showcasing
shoe fashions through the centuries.

The Shoe Museum

Clarks Village,
Street,
Somerset BA16 0YA
+44 (0)1458 842 169
A collection of shoes dating from
Roman times to the present day,
together with machinery used in
footwear production and information
on the history of the famous Clark
family and its connection with the
development of shoemaking in Street.

Victoria and Albert Museum

Cromwell Road,
London SW7 2RL
+44 (0)20 7942 2000
www.vam.ac.uk
Fashion and textile collection
dating from the seventeenth
century to the present day, with
an emphasis on influential
European design. Also
showcases accessories such
as shoes, gloves and jewellery.

UNITED STATES

The Costume Institute

The Metropolitan Museum of Art,
1000 Fifth Avenue at 82nd Street,
New York, NY 10028–0198
+1 212 535 7710
www.metmuseum.org
Vast collection of 80,000 costumes,
including shoes and accessories.

Vintage Fashion Museum

212 North Broadway,
Abilene, KS 67410
+1 785 263 7997
www.abilenekansas.org
Fashions from the 1870s to
the 1970s, with a large collection
of shoes and other accessories.

CANADA

The BATA Shoe Museum

327 Bloor Street West,
Toronto, Ontario M5S 1W7
+1 416 979 7799
Hundreds of shoes (from a
collection of over 10,000 pairs)
on display, celebrating 4,500
years of footwear from Chinese
bound foot shoes to glamorous
1970s platforms.

Costume Museum of Canada

109 Pacific Avenue,
Winnipeg, Manitoba
+1 204 989 0072
www.costumemuseum.com
Intended as a national repository
for costume, accessories and
textiles, the collection includes
pieces by many internationally
renowned designers

Stores and boutiques

UNITED KINGDOM

Absolute Vintage

15 Hanbury Street,
London E1 6QR
+44 (0)20 7247 3883
www.absolutevintage.co.uk

Appleby

95 Westbourne Park Villas,
London W2 5ED
+44 (0)20 7229 7772
www.applebyvintage.com
A friendly and accomodating vintage
boutique run by Jane Appleby-Deen.

Armstrongs

83 Grassmarket, Old Town,
Edinburgh EH1 2HJ
+44 (0)131 220 5557
www.armstrongsvintage.co.uk

Beyond Retro

58–59 Great Marlborough Street,
London W1 F7JY
+44 (0)20 7434 1406

Blackout II

51 Endell Street,
London WC2 9HJ
+44 (0)20 7240 5006
www.blackout2.com
A treasure trove, specializing in
the 1930s and 1940s.

Cenci

4 Nettlefold Place,
London SE27 0JW
+44 (0)20 8766 8564
www.cenci.co.uk

C20 Vintage Fashion

enquiries@c20vintagefashion.co.uk
www.c20vintagefashion.co.uk
Cleo and Mark Butterfield's
inspirational vintage garments and
shoes are available for hire.

Frock Me!

www.frockmevintagefashion.com
For vintage fashion fairs in London
and Brighton.

The Girl Can't Help It

Shop G100, G90 and G80,
Alfie's Antique Market,
13–25 Church Street,
London NW8 8DT
+44 (0)20 7724 8984
www.sparklemoore.com

Kitt's Couture

51 Chapel Street,
Penzance TR18 4AF
+44 (0)1736 350 240
www.kittscouture.co.uk

Marshmallow Mountain

Ground Floor, Kingly Court,
49 Carnaby Street,
London W1K 5AB
+44 (0)20 7434 9498
www.marshmallowmountain.com

One of a Kind

253/259 Portobello Road,
London W11 1LP
+44 (0)20 7792 5284

Palette London

21 Canonbury Lane,
London N1 2AS
+44 (0)20 7288 7428

The Real McCoy

21 The Fore Street Centre,
Fore Street,
Exeter EX4 3AN
+44 (0)1392 410 481
www.therealmccoy.co.uk

The Red Cross Shop

67 Old Church Street,
London SW3
+44 (0)845 0547 101

Rellik

8 Goldborne Road,
London W10 5NW
+44 (0)20 8962 0089

Retro

8 Otago Street,
Kelvinbridge,
Glasgow G3 8BW
+44 (0)141 221 4433
www.retro-clothes.com

Rokit

101 Brick Lane,
London E1 6SE
+44 (0)20 7375 3864
225 Camden High Street,
London NW1 7BU
+44 (0)20 7267 3046
42 Shelton Street,
London WC2 9HZ
+44 (0)20 7836 6547
www.rokit.co.uk

Steinberg & Tolkien

139 Kings Road,
London SW3 5ED
+44 (0)20 7376 3660

Studio 66

Unit 205, Westbourne Studios,
242 Acklam Road,
London W10 5JJ
+44 (0)20 8964 4749
www.studio66.co.uk

TopShop Vintage
214 Oxford Street,
London W1W 8LG
+44 (0)20 7636 7700
www.topshop.co.uk
Based in the Oxford Street branch in
London, contains a large collection of
vintage shoes and clothing.

UNITED STATES
Atomic Passion
430 East 9th Street,
New York, NY 10009
+1 212 533 0718
An amazing array of vintage and
antique footwear and clothing

Cherry
19 Eighth Avenue,
New York City, NY 10014
+1 212 924 1410
www.cherryboutique.com
The world's largest collection of
pristine, unworn vintage shoes.

Miami Twice
6562 Bird Road,
Southwest 40th Street,
Miami, FL 33155–4830
+1 305 666 0127
www.miami-twice.com

New York Vintage
117 West 25th Street
New York, NY 10001
+1 212 647 1107
newyorkvintage.com

The Paper Bag Princess
8818 Olympic Boulevard,
Beverly Hills, CA 90211
+1 310 385 9036
287 Davenport Road,
Toronto, Ontario M5R 1J9
www.thepaperbagprincess.com

Sasparilla
1630 Pennsylvania Avenue,
Miami Beach, FL 33139
+1 305 532 6611
Especially noted for shoes
by Charles Jourdan and Prada.

Star Shoes
6364 Hollywood Boulevard,
Los Angeles, CA 90028
+1 323 462 7827

A cocktail bar, shoe museum and
shop all in one place, specializing in
original box-fresh designs by Joseph
La Rose.

The Way We Wore
334 South La Brea Avenue,
Los Angeles, CA 90036
+1 323 937 0878
www.thewaywewore.com

CANADA
Divine Decadence Originals
136 Cumberland Street, Upper Floor,
Toronto, Ontario M5R 1A2
+1 416 324 9759
www.divinedecadence.sites.toronto.
com

Delux Junk Company
310 W Cordova Street,
Vancouver, BC V6B 1E8
+1 604 685 4871

Ego
9 Kensington Avenue,
Toronto, Ontario M5T 2J8
+1 416 596 8282

MaryAnn Harris
Ottawa Antique Market,
1179A Bank Street,
Ottawa, Ontario
+1 613 720 9242

AUSTRALIA
The Diva's Closet
10–11 Young Street,
Paddington,
Sydney, NSW 2021
+61 (0)2 9361 6659
By appointment only.

Vintage Clothing Shop
147–49 Castlereagh Street,
Shop 5, CBD,
Sydney 2000
+61 2 9267 7155

Online stores and resources
**1860–1960 One Hundred Years of
Fashion and Accessories**
www.1860–1960.com

Another Time Vintage Apparel
www.anothertimevintageapparel.com

Antique Lace & Fashion
www.antique-fashion.com

Ballyhoo Vintage
www.ballyhoovintage.com

Dandelion Vintage Clothing
www.dandelionvintage.com

Davenport and Company
www.davenportandco.com

eBay
www.ebay.com

Enokiworld
www.enokiworld.com

FashionDig.com
www.fashiondig.com

Incogneeto Vintage
www.neetstuff.com

It's Vintage Darling
www.itsvintagedarling.com

Kitty Girl Vintage
www.kittygirlvintage.com

Midnight Sparkle
www.midnightsparklevintageclothing.
com

Nelda's Vintage Clothing
www.neldasvintageclothing.com

Posh Vintage
www.poshvintage.com

Retrodress
www.retrodress.com

Sydneys Vintage Clothing
www.sydneysvintageclothing.com

Vintage Martini
www.vintagemartini.com

Designers' websites
André Courrèges
www.courreges.com

Bruno Magli
www.brunomagli.it

Charles Jourdan
www.charles-jourdan.com

Christian Louboutin
www.christianlouboutin.fr

Gina Shoes
www.gina.com

Jimmy Choo
www.jimmychoo.com

Manolo Blahnik
www.manoloblahnik.com

Nicholas Kirkwood
www.nicholaskirkwood.com

Roger Vivier
www.rogervivier.com

Sergio Rossi
www.sergiorossi.com

Terry De Havilland
www.terrydehavilland.com

Vivienne Westwood
www.viviennewestwoodonline.co.uk

Glossary of Designers

Bally: Founded by Carl Franz Bally in 1851, the Swiss manufacturer had built an international reputation for quality and design in women's and men's footwear by the 1870s. His sons continued to develop the business after his death in 1899. From the 1920s, Bally shoes were successfully exported around the world, reaching a peak in the mid 1980s. Bally was sold to an American investment firm in 1999.

Biba: Ex-fashion illustrator Barbara Hulanicki set up Biba in 1964 to bring ready-to-wear fashion to a much younger demographic than that served by the long-established couture houses. Special importance was placed on the 'experience' of shopping at the London boutique, with the music turned up loud and shop girls instructed to never approach the customer. As the logo suggested, the main influences included Art Nouveau and Deco, and fantastical twists on the 1960s look. Brigitte Bardot, Twiggy, Yoko Ono, Sonny and Cher and Freddy Mercury all took to the look. Platforms in suede with the Biba 'Auntie' colours in mulberry, rust, black and purple were the order of the day. In 1975, the boutique closed, but the label was ironically reopened as a couture house under the auspices of designer Bella Freud. The look is now more luxe – 2008 sees metallic blacks and shiny patent leather – but some of the ornate patterns and the use of platform and doll-like round-toe Mary Jane styles have been reused.

Manolo Blahnik: After getting his first break in 1972 when fashion designer Ossie Clark asked him to make the shoes for a catwalk show, Spanish-born Blahnik has dominated shoe design and become world famous for his beautifully crafted, high-heeled shoes. In 1973 he set up his flagship store in London. Inspired by the work of Roger Vivier and other eras, such as the Regency or rococo periods, Blahnik is responsible for the design of every one of the thousands of shoes that bear his name.

Thea Cadabra: Cadabra learnt her trade while working for a Turkish shoe-maker in London, and applied these skills to make her wild, fantastical glam-rock designs. In 1976 she began her own workshop, having begun to receive commissions, and made shoes for the Crafts Council. Eventually she moved to France to work for Charles Jourdan. She currently lives in the US. Her designs often went far beyond the scope of the average shoe, employing heavy use of outlandish embellishment, such as her dragon-headed high-heeled pumps from the early 1980s.

Pierre Cardin: Known for his avant-garde designs in the 1960s, Cardin first launched a low-heeled square-toed boot in autumn 1961. He was one of the designers who championed the boot when it came back into fashion in the late 1960s, paired with a miniskirt. His assexual clothing designs were worn with thigh-high boots and space-age shift dresses.

Jimmy Choo: Born into a family of Malaysian shoemakers and a true master of the craft, Choo graduated from Cordwainers College in London and the London College of Fashion. It wasn't long before Princess Diana became Choo's best client for bespoke footwear. In 1996 he went into partnership with Tamara Mellon, formerly of British *Vogue*, and launched a ready-to-wear line of shoes. In April 2001, he sold his 50 per cent stake in the company and has since been concentrating on the exclusive Jimmy Choo Couture line.

Robert Clergerie: After buying the shoe company Fenestrier in 1978, the French designer debuted his eponymous line in 1981 with lace-up Oxfords, a man's shoe made for a woman that has since become a classic. He also designed the raffia sandal in 1992 and the 'parallelogram' heel in 1984. Clergerie's shoes are known to be wearable as well as beautiful, and his unornamented, strong clean designs won him the *Footwear News* Designer of the Year awards in 1987 and 1990.

André Courrèges: The French designer is credited with inventing the miniskirt and introducing the Go-Go boot to the world, which was a white, low-heeled boot, rising just above the ankle. He pioneered cut-out boots, which first appeared in 1964 along with his first 'space age' black-and-white fashion collection.

Patrick Cox: In his first year at Cordwainers College in London, Cox designed platform shoes for Vivienne Westwood's 1984 Witches collection and went on to create for John Galliano, Workers for Freedom and Anna Sui. He set up on his own in 1985, designing street-smart footwear and becoming known for his use of unusual materials such as chain mail. His most successful design was the Wannabe loafer in 1993, a colourful revival of the hush-puppies classic. He spent two years as creative director for Charles Jourdan in the early 2000s.

David Evins: English-born Evins grew up in the US. After being fired as an illustrator for *Vogue*, he went to work as an pattern maker, then set up Evins Inc in New York and started designing with I Miller. In 1949 he was considered the 'King of Pumps' for his design of the shell pump, which revealed toe cleavage. He also promoted himself as a bespoke shoemaker, making shoes for film stars, including Claudette Colbert and Elizabeth Taylor. In the late 1950s he went into partnership with the Mario Valentino factory in Italy, designing for Valentino, Balenciaga, Bill Blass, Oscar de la Renta and others.

Salvatore Ferragamo: Ferragmo's scientific and creative approach to shoes spawned innovations such as the famous 'cage heel', and his company is now the largest exporter of high-end footwear in Italy. After starting a business in the US making shoes for film stars during the 1920s, he returned to Italy where he began to fashion shoes for the wealthiest and most powerful women. He was always recognized as a visionary, and his designs ranged from the strikingly bizarre objects d'art to the traditionally elegant.

Maud Frizon: Having launched her handmade shoes in 1970, this former fashion model created luxury feminine shoes and was known for her cone heel. Frizon's famous clientele included Brigitte Bardot, who wore her high-heeled Russian boots. Prominent in the late 1970s and 1980s, she designed for Azzedine Alaïa, Claude Montana, and Thierry Mugler as well as under her own labels Miss Maud and Maud Frizon.

Gina: Turkish shoemaker Mehmet Kurdash began his label Gina Shoes in 1954 in a basement in Shoreditch, and named it after his favourite film star, Gina Lollobrigida, to suggest glamour and beauty. His three sons have taken over the management, and Gina has dressed the feet of Madonna, Penelope Cruz and Nicole Kidman. Gina shoes are famous for their sculptural yet feminine quality, and a refusal to compromise on the excellence of materials.

Daniel Green: Green was a young freelance shoe salesman in 1881 when he visited the Dolgeville Felt Mill in New York. Taking his cue from the workers, who wore waste piano felt on their feet to keep them warm, Green struck a bargain with the Mill to produce these slippers en masse, for him alone to sell. By 1885 the company was selling 75,000 pairs, and the company continues to make slippers to this day.

Guccio Gucci: Taking his inspiration from the tailored English 'horsey' style, Gucci founded a saddlery in Florence in 1921 and branched out into luggage. The business rapidly expanded and in 1953 he opened a store in New York. The luxury brand first designed shoes in the 1930s, and in 1957 introduced a moccasin-constructed shoe with a gilded snaffle. It was originally available only for men until 1989 when a scaled-down version for women was introduced. During the 1950s, Gucci also developed the trademark striped webbing, which was derived from the saddle girth.

Terry de Havilland: Terry started by working his father's business making winklepinker boots during the 1960s. His career really took off after he reinterpreted a pair of 1940s platform wedge shoes in patchwork snakeskin. The rock 'n' roll crowd loved them and soon he was selling to clients such as Bianca Jagger, Cher and David Bowie, going on to open his own boutique on London's Kings Road. De Havilland was also instrumental in reintroducing the stiletto heel in the 1970s. When his store closed he launched a line called Kamikaze Shoes that featured winklepicker stilettos. Terry emerged with new partners in 2004 to re-launch the Terry De Havilland brand.

Charles Hellstern: Founded in Paris by Louis Hellstern in 1872, the Hellstern company created some of the best quality men's footwear available. Hellstern soon became known for its women's shoes and was patronized by the same clients as the top couturiers. Under Louis' son, Charles, the company became hugely successful in the 1920s, producing T-strap, plain pumps and instep strappy shoes. The company made leather shoes throughout the Second World War but business declined after the war ended.

Jan Jansen: In 1969 Dutch-born Jansen created the Woody clog, a new look for the Dutch *clompen*, with a leather upper fastened by nails to a wooden sole. It was copied by other manufacturers, eventually paving the way for the return of the clog in the 1970s. His high-healed sneaker of the late 1970s sold a million pairs in the US alone. Sensing a changing mood at the end of the twentieth century, he developed the Linea Erotica in the 1990s – shoes with a more sensual appeal. He has been selling under his own name since 1964.

Charles Jourdan: Originally trained as a shoemaker during the First World War, the French designer opened a shoe shop in Romans, France in 1919. By the time Charles's three sons took over the business in 1957, it already had a reputation for high-quality ready-to-wear women's footwear. The company was the first of its kind to advertise in premier fashion magazines, and so it linked Jourdan's shoes with that of the haute couture scene. Further prestige came from collaborations with Christian Dior and Pierre Cardin. After Jourdan's death in 1976, his sons ran the company, and Roland Jourdan took the reins in design. This brought a sense of innovation and the use of surrealist Guy Bourdin's photography in advertising the shoes cemented this reputation.

Beth and Herbert Levine: A former shoe model, Beth met and married journalist Herbert Levine and together they started a shoe company in 1948, with Beth heading the design side. The company introduced the world to Spring-O-Lator mules and stocking boots, and also popularized the return of the boot in the mid 1960s. Fun heels, rhinestone-covered pumps and the use of new materials such as vinyl and acrylic were trademarks of the Levine look. Crazy styles included paper shoes, sandals with Astroturf insoles and upper-less sandals. The company closed in 1975.

Christian Louboutin: Inspired by cabaret showgirls, Louboutin describes himself as a bit of a shoe fetishist. He trained at Charles Jourdan and sold freelance designs before opening his own shop in 1991 in Paris. Louboutin shoes feature a signature red sole – all are painted red, whatever their upper colour – and the top lifts of his heels are often shaped to leave rosette imprints. He calls these his 'follow me' shoes. Women ranging from Angelina Jolie to Mariah Carey and Christina Aguilera are fans of his shoes and many celebrities now choose his shoes to wear on the red carpet.

André Perugia: Perugia's talents as a shoemaker were spotted by Paul Poiret, who set him up in Paris in 1921. Drawing inspiration from modern art, industry design and the Orient, his client list quickly grew to include starts from film and the Folies Bergère, such as Josephine Baker. In 1930, he entered into a collaboration with Elsa Schiaparelli. In 1937, he moved his shop to 2 rue de la Paix, where he would remain for the rest of his career, designing under his own label as well as for Rayne and I Miller in the US. In 1942 he registered a patent for an articulated wooden sole that was used during the wartime leather shortages, and in 1956 one for interchangeable heels.

Cesare Paciotti: Cesare's father, Giuseppe Paciotti, founded the Italian company specializing in handmade shoes in 1948, and in 1980 Cesare took over the business launching the Cesare Paciotti brand with the help of his sister Paola. Having created shoes for Gianni Versace, Romeo Gigli, Dolce & Gabbana and Roberto Cavalli, the company expanded the women's collections in the 1990s. Relying on experimental production techniques and quality materials, they have since launched Paciotti 4US, a unisex sport and leisure shoe line.

Andrea Pfister: In 1936 this Italian designer won Best International Footwear Designer for his snakeskin pump, called Comedie. By 1964 he was designing for Jean Patou and Lanvin. He opened his first boutique in Paris, and after expanding into bags and belts, opened a second in Milan in 1987. Pfister, a master of colour and applied decoration, is known for adorning his shoes with sumptuous embroidery, skins and sequins. His opulent creations have been described as frivolous, witty, and even in dubious taste, yet the success of his creations depends on the combination of proportion and line with comfort.

François Pinet: The son of a French provincial shoemaker, Pinet is thought of as the first great shoe designer to make a name for himself, creating for the fashionable elite from his shop in Paris which opened in 1855. Pinet's reputation rose as haute couture became established and he is credited with popularizing the return of the high heel in the 1870s. His trademark high Louis heel became known in the late nineteenth century as the 'Pinet heel'.

Miuccia Prada: Born in 1947, Miuccia, the youngest granddaughter of Prada founder Mario Prada, took over the family-owned luxury goods manufacturer in 1978. Since then, she and her husband Patrizio Bertelli have turned it into a fashion powerhouse, acquiring Jil Sander, Helmut Lang and shoemaker Church & Co. In 1992, she debuted the less expensive Miu Miu (Miuccia's nickname), inspired by her personal wardrobe.

Mary Quant: Crowned the 'High Priestess of Sixties Fashion' by the journalist Bernard Levin, Quant was famous for her miniskirt designs. The Swinging London look relied on the stacked heels and platforms, which set off the petite, childlike clothing styles and bold, primary colours and materials. Quant began designing shoes for Rayne in 1960, producing stilettos and ankle-strap shoes, and then went on to design her own range.

Edward Rayne: At age 28, Edward Rayne was still young when he took control of the family firm, founded in the 1880s. The first Rayne shoe store had opened in 1920 on New Bond Street in London and was granted a royal warrant by Queen Mary in the mid 1930s. French and Italian design led the field in the 1950s but Rayne, from early on in his career, took an interest in promoting British design. After producing shoes with Delman in the US for the British market, he signed a deal with Genesco in 1957 to produce Roger Vivier-designed Christian Dior shoes. He also created shoe collections for fashion designers including Hardy Amies, Mary Quant, Bruce Oldfield and Jean Muir.

Sergei Rossi: The son of an Italian shoemaker, Rossi began working with his father in the 1950s. In 1966 he moved to Milan to begin selling his own footwear. His biggest seller was the Opanca shoe, which took from his ideal of a natural, comfortable relationship between shoe and foot with a sole that blended into the upper. By the 1970s Rossi was collaborating with Gianni Versace. Business boomed and he opened two new boutiques each year between 1980 and 1999. He subsequently worked with Dolce & Gabbana and Azzedine Alaïa in the 1990s. Famous for his statuesque heel, always at least 7.5 cm (3 inches) high, today the brand is led by Edmundo Castillo, and emphasizes feminine sexuality with spike heels, vibrant jewel-like colours and shiny patent leathers.

Elsa Schiaparelli: A contemporary of Coco Chanel, Schiaparelli took inspiration from the prevalent Surrealist movement in the 1930s and created playful, witty and experimental designs. Her eccentric footwear included the 5 cm (2 inch) wedge-soled shoe and monkey-fur shoes from 1938, trimmed so that the fur sweeps the ground by the heels. A collaboration with Dalí produced a felt shoe-shaped hat. Although *Time* magazine named Schiaparelli 'a genius', she was superseded in popularity by Coco Chanel, largely because her preference for architectural, anti-body shapes made her unwilling to adapt to the post-war fashions.

Walter Steiger: Swiss-born, Paris-based Steiger has been designing shoes since the 1960s when he designed the collection Bally Medeleine and produced shoes for Mary Quant, after which he presented his first collection under his own name in 1967. With a faithful celebrity client base, he has also created shoes for Emanuel Ungaro, Claude Montano, Karl Lagerfeld, Kenzo, Azzedine Alaïa, Bill Bass, Oscar de la Renta and Calvin Klein.

Seymour Troy: Polish-born Troy opened a factory under his name in the US in 1923 and later produced a line called Troylings. He was responsible for originating half sizes, the creation of a shankless shoe, asymmetric strap closures and the much-copied high-cut shoe called Valkyrie. He was given the first Mercury Award from the National Shoe Industry Association (NSIA) in 1960 in recognition of 35 years of pioneering design.

Roger Vivier: Perhaps the most innovative shoe designer of the twentieth century, the French designer Vivier maintained an eye for the cutting edge of fashion for six decades. His shoes have been worn by such prestigious names as Diana Vreeland, the Queen of England, and Marlene Dietrich. He opened his first store in 1937 in rue Royale, Paris and his platform shoe went on to be used by Elsa Schiaparelli in her 1939 collection. In 1953 he created a line of prêt-a-porter shoes for Delman–Christian Dior label. In 1955 the label changed to 'Dior created by Vivier', the first time a shoe designer appeared alongside a couturier on a label. Vivier perfected his variations of the stiletto heel while working with Dior, and was an innovator with toes and heels during this period, popularizing the stiletto and introducing the 'comma' heel in 1962. In 1963 he opened his own design studio in Paris and created his signature line. His association with Paris couture, however, continued until 1972 with designs for Chanel, Hermès and Yves Saint Laurent. Between 1972 and 1993 Vivier went into semi-retirement but worked right up until his his death in 1998.

Stuart Weitzman: Weitzman's father, Seymour Weitzman, started a shoe factory in Massachusetts in the late 1950s, called Seymour Shoes. When he died, Stuart, who was working as a pattern cutter, inherited the business. In 1982 his clear Lucite Cinderella pump sold more than 70,000 pairs. *Brides* magazine in 1987 honoured him with IRIS Award for Excellence and for revolutionizing bridal footwear. Especially popular was his Sheer Delight pump of embroidered lace. Stuart has built a reputation for using unique materials, including cork, 24-carat gold, vinyl and hand-painted python. He is also known for sculpted heels that sometimes use materials like chrome, steel or bamboo. In 1990s he became one of leaders of retro style when he reintroduced the Louis-heeled pump and boot in 1993, and in 1995 the 1960s square-toed low-heeled pump.

Vivienne Westwood: British fashion designer Westwood began designing shoes while working with Malcolm McLaren in the 1970s in London's burgeoning punk scene. After establishing her own label in 1980, she continued to design footwear for her collections. Her creations featured towering heels and curving platforms in bold shapes or outlandish reinterpretations of classic silhouettes. She regularly uses unusual colours and fabrics or exaggerated shapes and decorates her shoes with bows, buckles, ties and laces, often in unexpected places or combinations.

Pietro Yanturni: At the beginning of the twentieth century, master shoemaker Yanturni was crafting hand-crafted, exquisite shoes, which took years to create. His Paris shop sign was said to proclaim him as the 'most expensive shoemaker in the world'. He received first order in 1914 and remained in business until 1930, when the Depression made it difficult to sell bespoke luxury footwear. His shoes fitted perfectly, were light as a feather and were made of sumptuous materials such as lace, velvet and brocade.

Index

Figures in italics indicate captions to illustrations.

A

Abba 148
Abstract Expressionism 128, 196
Adam and the Ants 189
Adrian 57, 74
afternoon shoes 20
Aksham shoes *201*
Alaïa, Azzedine 184, 185, 190, *190*
Alice in Wonderland 39
American Film Corporation 68
Amies, Hardy 76, *93*
Anaconda tannery 184
Andy's of London *163*
Aniston, Jennifer 143
ankle straps 61, *79, 102, 150*, *159, 161, 163, 190, 206*
Annello and Davide 121
Antiqua Casa Crespo 148
Antonioni, Michelangelo 185
Argence, Alfred 52
Arlequinade shoes 49
Arletty 72
Arnold, William *15*
Art Deco 31, *34*, 42, 50, *55*, 57, 58, *64*, 67, 152, 159, *176*
Art Nouveau *121*
Assous, André 148
Astaire, Fred 58
Astroturf shoes 140, *140*
Atkinson, Bill *111*
Austen, Jane 72
Avaro, Rodolfo *163*
Avengers, The (television) 137

B

Baby Burlesk (film) 39
Bacall, Lauren 169
Bailey, David 116, 137, 169
Bakelite 34, 83
Baker, Josephine 49
Balenciaga 166, 196, *205*
Balian, Sarkis del 52
ballet pumps/flats 111, *113*, 145, 186
Ballet Russes 11
Bally 17, 123
Bally, Carl Franz 17

Bally Studio, Kings Road, London 185
Balmoral boots *see* Oxford shoes
bar shoes 37, *38*, *42*, 52, *54*, 58
bar straps *38*, *54*
Barbarella (film) 139
Barbie 103
Bardot, Brigitte 111, 139
Barnovi *58*
Battani 136
Bauhaus 31
Bazaar, London 116, 191
beadwork *23*, 25, *25*, 32, 34, 49, 52, *127*, 180
Beat collection 137
Beat Generation 111
Beatles, the 121
Beatnik style 111, 137
Beauvoir, Simone de 105
Behar, Henry 156
Belle de Jour (film) 119
Belle Epoque 8, 24, 169
Belle Otero, La 24–5
Bene wedges 159
Bensoussan, Robert 201
Bentivegna *86*
Berry, Halle 106, 201, *206*
Beth's Bootery (at Saks Fifth Avenue) 140
Biba 121, 144, 152–5, 159
Biba and beyond 146–71
Birdcage boutique, Nottingham 159
Birkenstock, Konrad 143
Birkenstock 143
Birkenstock Arizonas 143
Birkin, Jane 169
Birtwell, Celia 116
Bizarre magazine 137
Blackman, Honor 137
Blahnik, Evangelista 169
Blahnik, Manolo 8, 9, *158*, 160, 165, 166–9, 180, *182*, 192, 195, 201, *201*
Blake, Lyman 16
Blake, Peter 128
Blass, Bill 140, 185
Bloomingdale's department store, New York 169, 173
Blow-Up (film) 185
Boardman, Eleanor *41*
Bodymap 189, 191, 194
Bolan, Marc 156
Boone, Cliff *190*
'bootlegging' 45, *45*

boots: ankle 12, 61, 67, *67*, *68*, 72, *116, 131*, 132, 161, *182*, 184, 185, *190*, 192, *193, 196*; Balmoral *29*; Beatle 121, 13; biker 173; bondage 161; button 9, 18, 24–5, *24, 29*; calf-length *131*; Chelsea 121, 132; cowboy 162; *cuissarde* 138, *138*, 139, *144*; Dr Marten (DMs) 191, *193*, 195; Ferragamo 68; fetish 52, 159; Go-Go 136, *136*, 140; golf *23*; granny *152*; jongler *134*; kinky 137–9; knee-length 123, *139*, *152*, 192; laced 24, *24*, 25, *29*, 137, *152*; low-heeled 15. 132; men's *28*, *29*; Odyssey *198*; opera *18*; pirate 189, *189*; pixie *182*, 189; 'Quant-a-Foot' *131*; Russian 45, *45, 86*; space age *125, 133*; stocking 140, *140*; thigh-length 140, 192; Ugg 45; Wellington 45
Botticelli, Sandro: 'Birth of Venus' 57
bottiers (shoemakers) 18, 52, 96
Bourdin, Guy 160
Bow, Clara 68
Bowie, Angie 159
Bowie, David 147, 156, 159
Bowler, Moya 121
Boy George 189
Breton, André 67
Brevet Perugia label *90*
Brevitt 100
Brick shoes *166*
British Crafts Council *163*
brocade *54*
brogueing perforations 45, *45*
brogues *154*
Brooks, Donald *127*
brothel creepers 191, *191*
Brown, George Warren 39
Brown Shoe Company 39
Bruges style 208
Bruni, Carla 202
buckles *26*, *28*, 37, 72, 123: Art Deco 52; button- *94*; chrome 186; diamanté *125, 155*; diamond-studded 19; enamelled 50; front-fastening *61* gilt 23; jewelled *32*; marcasite

23, 42; metal *68*, 159; pearl-studded *34*, 52; sequined *127*; silver 119, *119*; square *32*; steel *20*, 23, *23*, 42
Buffalo trainers 191
Buñuel, Luis 119
Burstein, Joan 166
'Buster Brown' cartoon strip 39
butterfly shoes *178*
button-bar shoes *32*, *34*

C

Cadabra, Thea 162, *163*
Callot-Soeurs 11
Campbell, Naomi 190, 195, 202
Candie 148
canvas shoes 15
Capezio *84*, 111, 119
Capezio, Salvatore 111
Capri *113*
Capri pants/trousers 103, 111, *111*, *113*
Cardin, Pierre 92, 108, *116*, 132, *138*, *144*, *150*
Career Girl *134*
Carnaby Street style 128
Castelbajac, Jean-Charles de 186
Castillo, Edmund 202
Castle, Irene and Vernon 26, *26*
Chalayan, Hussein 196
Chanel, Coco 31, 72, 116, 173, 174, *174*, *175*, 213
Charisse, Cyd 103
Chassis shoes 159
Chelsea Cobbler 156
Chelsea Girl boutiques 121
Cher 147, 151, 159
chinoiserie 34
Chloé shows 196
choc ('shock') heels 97, *97*, 123
Choi, Sandra 201
Choo, Jimmy 9, 195, 196, 201, *201*
chopines 72
Christie shoes *198*
Christopher Robin (character) 39, 128
City Lights Studio shoes *150*
city shoes 90, *94*
Clark, Ossie 116, *139*, 147, 166, *166*, 169

Clark, Rose *86*
Clarke, Adele 196
cleaning shoes 213
Cleopatra (film) 61
Clergerie, Robert *175*
Cleverly, George *154*
Clint Eastwood collection 189
Clobber 121
clogs 147, 148, *171*
Cloud and Rainbow shoes 162
coats *37*, 115, *134*, 137
Cobain, Kurt 195
Cobblers to the World, Kings Road, London 159
Cocteau, Jean 169
Colbert, Claudette 61
collecting 211, 213
'Colleen' Utility shoes *76*
College Girl 136
Coltellacci, Giulio 139
Columbo, Joe 132
Commes des Garçons 186, *186*
Cooch Behar, Maharani of *74*
Cordalli-Royal label *121*
Corfam 119
Coty Award 140
Countdown 121
Courrèges, André 132, *133*, 134, 136, 184, 211
court shoes 2, 15, *42*, 61, *62*, *64*, *71*, 90, 96, 108, *112*, *163*, *175*, *176*, *178*, *190*, 195
see also pumps
Cox, Patrick 186, 189, 191
Crescent, Fracine 160
Crockett and Jones *29*
Cromwell shoes *17*, *28*
Cubism 31, 32, 34, 50, *55*

D

Dalí, Salvador 67
dancing shoes 26, *26*, 32, 37, 111, *144*
day shoes 20, *28*, 37, *54*, *62* *94, 112*
de Havilland, Terry 8, 147, 151, 159, *159*, 160, 193, 196, *196*, 211
de la Renta, Oscar 185
De Mille, Cecil B 68
Deacon, Giles 106
Delman *32*, 61, *93*, 123, 134
Delman, Herman 61, 74, 96, 98

Deneuve, Catherine 119
denim *170*
Diaghilev, Sergei 11
Diana, Princess 201, 206
Dietrich, Marlene 61, 74,
   97, 206
Dior, Christian 18, 74, 90, *93*,
   96, 97, 98, 108, 115, *119*,
   123, *127*, 137, *155*, *178*,
   206, 211
Dolce & Gabbana 202
Dolcis *98*, 100, 148, 151, *170*
Dolly shoes 186
Dolly Sisters *26*
Donen, Stanley 111
Donna magazine 58
Doon, Bonnie *134*
Doucet 11
Dragon shoes 162
dress for success (1980s)
   172–93
dresses: bandage *190*;
   cocktail 31, *34*, 180;
   dance 32; dinner *86*; drop-
   waisted *54*, *55*; halterneck
   113, 147; knitted wool
   90; Laura Ashley 147;
   maxi 147; mini 115, 190,
   192; pinafore 116, 137;
   puff *165*; sheath 93; shift
   174; sleeveless *41*, *84*;
   spaghetti-strapped 50; tea
   195; tubular *50*; velvet *61*
driving shoes 140
Dumer, Ruth *125*
Dupont 119
Dupré, Jean-Pierre 184
Duran Duran 189
Durbin, Karen 105

E
Earth shoes *150*, 151
eco philosophy *150*
Edwardian elegance (1900–
   19) 10–29
Ekberg, Anita 159
Ekland, Britt 159
Elias, Eileen 24
Elizabeth II, Queen 96, *125*
Elle magazine *185*
Ellis, Perry 169, *182*
embroidery 20, 23, 24, *25*,
   49, *65*, 123, *127*: gold
   threadwork 19; Moroccan
   131; Rococo revival *18*,
   19, 25
Emms, Robert 161

ergonomics 50, 72
espadrilles 148, *148*, *150*,
   168
Espart 148
Esperento *182*
Evelyn, Fay 23
evening shoes 20, *23*, 29,
   32, *34*, 37, *39*, *54*, *55*, *86*,
   140, *202*
Evins, David 61, *61*, 72, *127*,
   134
Exposition des Arts
   Décoratifs (Paris, 1924) 31

F
Fatal Ring, The (film) *24*
feathered shoes 19
Fellini, Federico 159
Fellowes, Daisy 67
Feraud, Louis *144*
Ferragamo, Salvatore 8,
   68–71, 72, 74, *74*, *75*, 76,
   79, 80, *80*, 83, 84, *87*, 89,
   98, 100, *100*, *131*, 173,
   202, 211
Festival of Britain (1951) 93
'Fetish' art installation (Paris,
   2007) 208
fetishism 137, 140, 161, 162
Fiorentina, Silvia 162
First World War 15, *16*, 17,
   23, *23*, 49
Fitz-Simon, Stephen 152
Fitzgerald, F Scott 52
flappers 31, *32*, *34*, 37, *37*,
   39, 45, 52
flat shoes 9, 111, 115, 121,
   128, *145*, 186, 189
Flett, John 186
Florsheim 16, *86*
Fluevog, John *156*
Foale, Marion 121
footbed shoes 143
Folie shoes 49
Fonda, Jane 139
footbed shoes 143
'footwear couture' 18
Footwear magazine 89
Ford, Tom 195
Foster, Jodie *170*
Fraser, Margot 143
Frederick's of Hollywood 103
French, John *98*
Freud, Sigmund 11
Friedan, Betty 105
Frizon, Maud 8, 180, 184,
   184, 192
Frost French 159

Funny Face (film) 111
future collectables 194–213

G
Gainsbourg, Serge: 'Harley
   Davidson' 139
gaiters 29
gaiters-cum-legwarmers *197*
Galanos 140
Galerie Lafayette 166
galoshes 37, *37*, 45
Gardner, Ava 61, 105
Garland, Judy 61, 72, *75*
garters *26*, *43*
Gaultier, Jean-Paul 189, *190*,
   191, *191*
Gazette du Bon Ton
   magazine *42*, *50*
Geiger, Kurt 134
Gentlemen Prefer Blondes
   (film) 8, *100*
Ghesquière, Nicolas 196
ghillies 186
Giacometti, Alberto 93
Gilda (film) 61
Gilet, A 52
Gina Shoes 105, *105*, 106,
   106, *121*, 160, *174*, *176*,
   178, 193, *198*, *199*
Ginsberg, Allen 111
Girl from Cooks, The 37
glam rock 147, 156, *156*, *196*
Glamour magazine 103
Glen of Michigan *111*
Glitter Band 156
golf shoes 189
Golo Boots 136
Goodman, Georgina 196
Goody Two Shoes 156
Gough, John 137
Grable, Betty 83
grandes horizontales
   (courtesans) 8, 24
Great War *see* First World War
Greco 58
Greece, Princess of 19
Green, Daniel 25
griffes (signatures) 18, *50*,
   97, *123*
Gucci Group 173, 195, 202,
   205
Guge shoes *166*

H
H&M Rayne *103*
Hall, Jerry *165*, 180
Halston 140, 165, *165*

Hamilton, Richard 128
Hamnett, Katherine *174*, *192*
Hardie, Miss *38*
Hardy, Pierre 196
Harlow, Jean 57
Harper's Bazaar magazine
   67, 90
Harris, Gretchen *111*
Harrods department store,
   London 173
Hartnell, Norman *93*
hats 31, *32*, *55*, *90*
Hays code 57
Hayworth, Rita 61, *61*
heels: ball 123; block *95*,
   128, *145*, 152; celluloid
   52; *choc* ('shock') 97,
   123; comma 97, *123*, *161*,
   185, *193*; cone 9, 180,
   180, *192*, 196; crystal *134*;
   Cuban 17, 31, 32, 45, *55*,
   116, 121, *144*, *155*, 189,
   196; escargot 123; gem-
   studded *127*; globe *127*;
   kitten 116, *127*, 128, *145*;
   Lucite 58; needle 98, 108,
   123, *123*, *178*; Perspex
   206, *208*; Pinet 18, 19;
   platform 76, 83, *87*, 147,
   195, 196, *208*; pyramid
   123; Sabrina 116; spool
   87, 123; square 119, 121,
   155; stacked 37, *145*, *170*;
   stem 97; stiletto 8, 49, *68*,
   90, 97, 98–103, 105, *105*,
   106, 115, *123*, *127*, 140,
   147, 160–65, *174*, *180*,
   185, *188*, 189, *190*, *192*,
   195; tapered 37, *39*, *84*,
   98, *102*, *178*; wedge 8,
   68, 71, *72*, 76, 79, *79*, *80*,
   83, *87*, 159, *161*, *170*, *174*,
   193, 211; wheel *105*
   see also Louis heels
Hellstern 52, *52*
Hemingway, Wayne and
   Geraldine 189
Hepburn, Audrey 111, *113*
Hepburn, Katharine 58
Heresco 186
Hermès 173
Herzigova, Eva 190
Hi Brow 136
hippie movement 111, 143,
   150, 152, *170*
Hitler, Adolf 57
Holah, David 189

Hollywood heel 56–87
Hook Knowles and Co. *23*
Hope, Emma 196
Hope Skillman *113*
Horst *58*, *113*
hot pants *156*, *170*
Hudson *116*
Hulanicki, Barbara 152
Hullabaloo (television) 136
Hutton, Laura *144*

I
I Magnin 134
I Miller Shoe Company 49,
   94, *108*, 123, 140
Institute of Footwear Design,
   Milan 184
International Surrealist
   Exhibition (London, 1936)
   67
invisible shoes *68*, 89, 140
Iran, Empress of 96

J
J & T Cousins *86*
jackets *16*, *55*, *61*, 137,
   160, 190
Jacobs, Marc 208, *211*
Jacobs, Dr Monroe 156
Jagger, Bianca 159, 165
Jagger, Mick 180
Jasperware 34
Jimmy Choo Couture 201
Johnson, Betsy *144*
Johnson, Jackie *131*
Jones, Grace 189
jongler boots *134*
Jourdan, Charles 9, 49, *90*,
   98, *108*, *108*, *116*, *119*,
   145, *148*, *155*, 160, *161*,
   174, *178*, *180*, *182*, *188*,
   192, 206
Jourdan, Rene 108
Jourdan, Roland 108
Joyce, Lynne 62
Julienne 52, *86*

K
Kamikaze Shoes 159
Kawakubo, Rei 186, *186*,
   190, 191
Keds 15
Kelly, Grace 61, 96
Kendal Milne *102*
Kenzo 185
Kerouac, Jack 111
Khan, Emmanuel 132

Kidman, Nicole 106
'Kinky Boots' (song) 137
Kirkwood, Nicholas 196, *196*
Klein, Calvin 185
Klum, Heidi 143
Kobe shoes 206
Kork-Ease 156
Kucuk shoes *201*
Kumagai, Tokio 186, *186*
Kurdash, Mehmet 105, 106, *106*

L
La Bal shoes 49
La Dolce Vita (film) 159
laced shoes *62*, *86*
Lagerfeld, Karl 173, *175*, 185
Laird and Schoeber 83
Lanvin, Jeanne 15, *90*, 184
Laura Ashley 147
leather: artificial 119; gold-embossed *121*; printed *112*; restrictions 62
Léger, Hervé 190
Legge, Sheila 67
Lennox, Annie 189
Leonard Lewis of Mayfair 115
Lestage, Nicholas 23
Levine, Beth 98, 103, 128, *131*, 140, *140*, 151, 211
Levine, Herbert *103*, *131*, 140
Liberty's of London *38*, *150*
Lichtenstein, Roy *196*
Lilley & Skinner 16, 100
loafers *111*, *117*, 173, *193*
Logan, Joshua *100*
Lollobrigida, Gina 106
Lotus shoes 134
Louboutin, Christian 8, 9, *196*, 206–9
Louis heels 9, 12, *12*, *16*, *17*, *18*, *18*, 19, 20, 23, *23*, 25, 26, *26*, *28*, 31, 37, *42*, *43*, 45, *52*, *62*, *71*, 97, 169, 180, 189
Louis XV, King of France 23, 68
Love, Bessie *37*
Love, Courtney 39, 195
Love shoes 206
Lucile, Lady Duff Gordon 18
Lydig, Rita de Acosta 19
Lynch, David 208

M
McCallum *86*
McCardell, Claire 74, 111

McCarthy, Eileen 103
Maceses *76*
McKinney, Henry Nelson 15
Macnee, Patrick 137
Madly 108
Madonna 195
Magli, Bruno *119*, *127*, *148*, 180
Maid shoes 162, *163*
Mansfield, Jayne 103, 105
Marcos, Ferdinand E. 173
Marcos, Imelda 173
Margaux shoes 159, *196*
Marie Claire magazine 185
Marikina City Footwear Museum, Manila 173
Martini Dry shoes 184
Mary Jane shoes *38*, *39*, *41*, *55*, 115, *116*, *145*
mass production 9, 16, 17, 18, 68, 71
Massaro, Sébastien 116
Maxim 108
Medici shoes 184
Méléard, Benoît *196*
Mellon, Tamara 201
Mexico Shoes 106
Michonet 25
Micia *131*
Midler, Bette 151
Miller, Israel 76
Miller, Sienna 159, *196*
Milne, A A: *Winnie the Pooh* 39
Minnelli, Liza 140, 165
Minogue, Kylie 195
Miracles: 'Going to a Go-Go' 136
Miranda, Carmen 79, *79*
Missoni *180*
Mistinguett 46, *46*
Mitford, Nancy 52
Miu Miu shoes *2*, 159, 208, 211
moccasins *155*
Modernist shoe (1920s) 30–55
Moke, Johnny 159
Molinard Bottier, Zurich 185
Molloy, John T: *Women: Dress for Success* 174
Mondrian, Piet 119, 162
Monroe, Marilyn 8, 74, 84, 100, *100*, 103, *198*
Montana, Claude 185
Moon Girl collection 132
Moore, Vida *32*

Morris, Olivia 196
Morton, Digby 76
Mosaique shoes 184
Moss, Kate 159, *196*
Mugler, Thierry 180, *180*, 184, 193
Muir, Jean 93, *125*, 151, 169
Mulberry 147
mules 25, 46, *50*, 57, 111, 169, 180, 186, *198*: high-heeled 103, *103*; Magnet 103, *108*; slide 148; spike-heeled 162; Spring-O-Lator 103, *103*, *113*, 160; stiletto *113*; Tomato 184; Trash 206; Zeta *199*
Mussolini, Benito 76, 98

N
Naked Lady shoes *163*
Naylor, Genevieve 95
Negresco hotel, Nice 49
Negri, Pola 49
Neiman Marcus Award 71
New Look shoes (1948–59) 88–113
New Romanticism *182*, 189
New York Herald 39
New York Times 18, 26, 156
Newton, Helmut 160, 202
Newton Elkin *61*
Nielsen, Brigitte 190
Nikes 180
Nirvana 195
North Pole collection 184
NW Ayer & Son 15

O
'Ode to Industry' shoes 50
Onassis, Jackie 74, 119
Op Art *105*, 128, *128*, *169*
opanke (moccasin) 111
Oppenheim, Meret: 'Le Dejeuner en Fourrure' 67
Orientalia shoes 180
Ossie shoes *166*
Outcault, Richard F 39
overshoes 37
Owen, Toni *94*
Oxford shoes 12, 45–6, *45*, *54*, *55*, 58, 62, *86*, 111, 166

P
Paciotti, Cesare 9, *196*
Padova of Paris 49, 67, *67*
Page, Bettie 103
Pallenburg, Anita 151

Palter DeLiso *112*, 140, *145*
Paltrow, Gwyneth 143
Panettiere, Hayden 148
Panton, Verner 132
Paolozzi, Eduardo 128
Paquin 11, 15
Parker, Sarah Jessica 195
Parkinson, Norman *2*, *83*, *116*, *117*, *125*, *128*, *148*, *165*
patent leather shoes *23*, 31, 46, *106*, *111*, 121, *155*, *161*, *163*, *168*, *174*, *180*, 205
Patou, Jean 184
pattens 72
Pavlova, Anna 111
Peacock *86*
Peeko Tie *86*
Penis shoes 189
Penrose Annual 24
Perils of Pauline, The (silent film serial) 24
Perry shoes *182*
Perugia, André 8, *45*, 46, 49–50, *49*, *50*, 62, *64*, *65*, *66*, 67, 72, *90*, 98, *98*, 169, 184
Peter Robinson department store, London 23
Pfister, Andrea 162, 180, 184, *184*, 192
Philipson, Stanley *145*
Piaggi, Anna *169*
Piaggi shoes *169*
Picasso, Paloma 166
Pickford, Mary 68
Pinet, Jean-Louis François 18, *18*, 19, 24, 50
Pinet Shoe Salon, Brompton Road, London *136*
Pirate Collection 189
plastic 128, 134, 140
platform shoes *148*, *150*, *152*, 156, *158*, 159, 160, 162, *163*, 169, 174, 206, 211: Rodita zip 206; Teeter 74
Platinum Blonde (film) 57
plimsolls 15
Poiret, Denise 49
Poiret, Paul 11, *12*, 15, 31, 49
Pollock, Alice *139*
Pompadour, Madame de 23
pop art 128, *140*, 156, 159, 186, *196*, 211
Poppy shoes *196*
Porter, Thea 147

Portrait collection 195
poulaines 19
'poverty chic' style 147
Powell and Moya 93
power dressing 174, 186
power shoes 174–9
Prada shoes 208
Premier 86
Premier, François 97
Premila, Princess, of Rajpipia *136*
Prezfelder, Mr *106*
Pucci, Emilio 202
Pugh, Gareth 106
pull-over shoes *68*
pumps 15, 76, *84*: ballet 111, *113*; beaded 96–7; block-heeled *95*; day *86*, *94*; evening 32, *34*, 140; flat 111, 186; Lily *127*; opera 93, *105*, *108*, *112*; Pilgrim 118–27, 145; Shell 61; tapered-heel *84*
see also court shoes
punk 160, 161, 162, *188*, 189
puttees 23
PVC (polyvinyl chloride) 128, 134, *144*

Q
Quant, Mary 115, 116, 121, 128, *131*, *144*, 185
Queen magazine 159
Queen Quality 68

R
Rabanne, Paco 132
Rainier, Prince, of Monaco 61
Rambaldi, A. *32*
Rampling, Charlotte 169
Ravel 134
Rawlings, John *2*
Rayne, Sir Edward 32, *93*, 119, 123, *125*
Rebe 97
Red or Dead 191
Rego, Paula 128
Rhodes, Zandra 160
Ricci, Nina 184
Riley, Bridget 128
'Riot Girls' 195
Roberts, Harry 105
Roberts, Julia 201
Rocket shoes 162
Rocking Horse *189*, 189
Rocky Horror Picture Show, The 160

Rococo revival style *18, 19*, 25
Rogers, Ginger 58
Rooke, James *163*
Rooster shoes 186
Rossi, Sergio *155*, 196, 202–5
Rowley and Oram 159
Roxy Music 156
Royal label *121*
Runnin' Wild show 32
Russian Constructivism 55

S

Sacha 134, *150*, *156*
Sachs, Maxwell 103
saddle shoes 111
Saint Laurent, Yves 97, 119, 137, 139, 151, *192*
St Louis World's Fair (1904) 39
Saks Fifth Avenue 49, 140
Salamander shoes *15*
Salon, Joseph 74
sandal-pumps *49*
sandals *2*, 58, *58*, 61, *61*, 65, *68, 71, 72, 74*, 75, *80, 86, 87, 102, 108, 113, 121, 143, 144*, 148, *148, 156*, 159, 173, *185*, 189 *192*, *199, 201, 202*: Birkenstock *143*; Dr Scholl 151, *171*; espadrille *80*; gladiator-style *143, 205*; Gruyère *169*; Kimo 89, *100*; Leyla wedge 159; Minnie Mouse 186; Opanca 202; Ring *182*
Saul, Roger 147
Savage collection *189*
Saval, Ted 79
Schiaparelli, Elsa 67, *67*, 72, 74, 80, *87, 134*
Schubert *100*
Scorsese, Martin *170*
Scott-James, Ann 89
Sears, Roebuck and Company 45
Séducta label *90, 94*, 108, *108, 182*
semi-Oxford shoes 46
Sex, Kings Road, London 161
Seven Year Itch, The (film) 100
Sex and the City (television) 166, 195

Shepherd, EH 39
Shoe and Leather Lexicon 37
shoe clips 34, *34*
Shoecraft *86*
Shoes to Eat series 186, *186*
shopping 211, 213
Shrimpton, Jean 116, 137, *145*
Sinatra, Nancy 140, *140*
Singer, Isaac 16
skirts: ballerina 89; bouffant; crinoline 96; hobble *12*; maxi 156; micro *117*, 138; miniskirts 115, *117, 136*, 139, 140; pencil 93, 160; Poiret-style 11, *12*, 15; thigh-high 132; 'war crinoline' 15, *16*
Skylon 93
slingback shoes *68*, 83–4, *83*, 123, 127, 145, 155, *156*, 161, 180, *182*, 185, 206
slip-on shoes 15, *15*, 186
slippers 8, 12, 17, 20, 25, *52, 58*, 61, 65, 140: boudoir 19, 20, 25; Chinese 74; Gilda *199*; Utility *76*
small feet 12, 72, 211
Smerling, Harold 156
Smith, Paul 159
Smith, Richard 156
snakeskin 151
sneakers 15, 186
soles: cork 156; 'flexura' *12*; opanke *131*; platform 52, 72–5, *87, 156, 171*; rubber 15, *17*, 80, *148*, 191
Sottsass, Ettore 196
space age styles 132–5, *198*
Space Baby collection 191
Spandau Ballet 189
spats *37*
spectator shoes 15, 45–6, *54, 86*
Spencer's of London *106*
Spice Girls 191
split-bar shoes *37*
Sports Car shoes 186
sports shoes 15, 37
Spring-O-Lator 103, *103, 113*, 160
Sprouse, Stephen 189
Stanton, Eric 137
Starke, Frederick 137
Starr, Jimmy 100
Stead and Simpson *32*
Stefania tannery 184

Steichen, Edward *41*
Steiger, Walter 162, 185, *185*
step-in shoes *86*
Stern's *86*
Stewart, Stevie 189
stock market crash (1929) 57
stockings 19, 37, *43*, 93, 115, *125*, 132, 195
Stokes, William Earl Douglas 19
strapped shoes *12*, *17, 25*, *32*, 41–2, *165, 178*
Streisand, Barbra 140
Studio 54 disco, New York 165
suits *84, 90, 133, 175*, 180, *192*
Surrealism 67, *67*, 76, 96
Swank, Hilary 201
Swanson, Gloria 45, 49, 68, 140
Swarovski *100, 119, 198, 199*
Sweater Girl 103
Sweet 156

T

T-bar shoes *32*, 41, *41*, 42, *42, 43*, 49, 50, *50, 55*, 58, *65, 123, 155, 161, 163*, *205, 206*
tabi (Japanese sandal) 89
taboo shoes 161
tango shoes 8–9, 26, *26, 202*
tango, the 26, *26*, 32
'tango teas' 26
Tatianna thong sandal *199*
Taxi Driver (film) *170*
Taylor-Young, Leigh *148*
tea gowns 20, 25
Temple, Shirley 39
tennis shoes *17*
Theodoracopulos, Betsy 140
'These Boots Are Made For Walking' 140
tights *117, 128, 134*, 160
Time magazine 140, 152, 186
Tod's 173, 193
'toe cleavage' 61
toes: broad 24; chisel 119, 136; closed 32, 39; decoration *193*; elongated *42*; long, narrow 19; peek-a-boo 159; peep-toe *178*, *182*, 184, *206*; 'platypus' 121, 186; pointed 20, *32*, *105*, 119; rounded 71, *80*,

86, 116, 121, *121, 170*, 191; square *18, 50, 86*, 108, 119; turned-up *134*
Top Gear 121
Traherne, Annie 159
trainer shoes 189, 191
Trigère, Pauline *84, 143*
Troulala shoes 208
trouser suits *133*
Troy, Seymour 58
Troylings 58
Tuffin, Sally 121
Tukka 193
Turlington, Christy *196*
Turner, Lana 105
Turner, Tina 190
Tutankhamen 31
Tuttin, Sally 121
Twiggy 9, 115, *116*, 132, *134*, 145, *152, 154*

U

Utility fashions *76*, 84, 90

V

Vaccan *171*
valenki (Russian boots) 45
Valentino 148, *190*
Valentino, Rudolph 68
vamps 26, *55*, 186: canvas 45; cutaway *65*; decorated 'collars' on 123; extended 28; high-cut *52*, *62*, 108; interlacing *68*; low-cut décolleté 61; open- *127*; suede 46; V-shaped *79*
Van Ravenstein, Appollonia 158
Vargas, Alberto 83
Vasarely, Victor 128
Velázquez, Diego 169
Versace, Donatella 202
Versace, Gianni 202, *205*
Very Prive style 208
Victoria, Queen 29
Victoria and Albert Museum, South Kensington, London 195
Vionnet, Madeleine 31, 57
Viudas shoe 180
Vive la Cocotte collection *196*
Vivier, Roger 8, 18, 72, 74, *93*, 96–7, *97*, 98, 100, 119, *119*, 121, *123, 127*, 139, 140, 169, 206, 211
Vogue 18, 61, *83*, 84, 93, 106, 116, *117, 125, 128*, 143, 160, 166, 169, 180, 201

Vreeland, Diana 84, 96, 166
Vuitton, Louis 173

W

Wagenheim, Chris von 160
Walk-Over *86*
Wallace Elliott Company 25
'war crinoline' 15, *16*
Warhol, Andy 165, 208
Waverley Shoes 159
wearing vintage shoes 211, 213
Wedgwood 34
Weinberg, Chester *119*
Weitzman, Stuart *205*
Westwood, Vivienne 106, 161, 162, *162, 188*, 189, *189*, 190, 195, *196, 197*
Whisky a Go-Go discotheque 136
White, Pearl *24*
wide feet 62
Wiener Werkstaette 17
Williamson, Matthew *196*
Willie, John 137
Windsor, Duchess of 61, 119
Winehouse, Amy 159, *196*
winklepickers 105, *105, 113*, 119, 145, 195
Winters, Shelley 84
Wintour, Anna 180
Witches collection 189
Worth, Charles Frederick 18, 25
Wrapped collection 186
Wright, Frank Lloyd: Solomon R Guggenheim Museum, New York City *166*

Y

Yamamoto, Kansai 147, *166*
Yamamoto, Yohiji 186, 190, 191, 193
Yanturni, Pietro 8, 18–19, *19*, 49, 50, 96
Young, Loretta *80*
youth revolution 114–45

Z

Zapata boutique, Chelsea 166, 169
Zebedee shoes 159
Ziegfeld Follies 32

Further Reading

The Art of the Shoe, Marie-Josephe Bossan, Parkstone Press, 2004.

Boutique, Marnie Fogg, Mitchell-Beazley, 2003.

The Glass of Fashion: A Personal History of Fifty Years of Changing Tastes and the People Who Have Inspired Them, Cecil Beaton, Cassell, 1954.

Heavenly Soles, Mary Trasko, Abbeville Press, 2007.

The Literary Companion to Fashion, Colin McDowell, Reed International, 1995.

Marilyn Monroe: The Biography, Donald Spoto, Chatto & Windus, 1993.

On Fair Vanity, Betty Page, Convoy Publications Ltd, 1954.

On Human Finery, Quentin Bell, Allison & Busby, 1992.

Patrick Cox: Wit, Irony and Footwear, Tamasin Doe, Thames & Hudson, 1998.

The Penguin Book of Twentieth-century Fashion Writing, Judith Watt, Penguin, 1999.

Red or Dead, Tamsin Kingswell, Watson-Guptil, 1998.

Roger Vivier, Colombe Pringle, Assouline, 2005.

The Seductive Shoe, Jonathan Walford, Stewart, Tabor and Chang, 2007.

Sergio Rossi, Anne-Marie Clais, Assouline, 2008.

The Sex Life of the Foot and Shoe, William A Rossi, Krieger Publishing Co, 1993.

Shoes, Linda Pratt and Linda Woolley, Victoria & Albert Museum, 1999.

Shoes: A History from Sandals to Sneakers, Giorgio Riello and Peter McNeil, Berg, 2006.

Shoes: A Lexicon of Style, Valerie Steele, Scriptum Editions, 2005.

Shoes: What Every Woman Should Know, Stephanie Pedersen, David & Charles, 2005.

Shops and Shopping 1800–1914, Alison Adburgham, Barrie & Jenkins, 1989.

Vivienne Westwood, Jane Mulvagh, HarperCollins, 2003.

Women: Dress for Success, John T Molloy, W Foulsham & Co Ltd, 1980.

Womens' Shoes in America 1795–1930, Nancy E. Rexford, Kent State University Press, 2000.

Author Acknowledgements

Thanks to the delightful Christian Louboutin and his staff especially Colette and Sonia in Paris and Anne in London, the UK's finest literary agent Sheila Ableman, Lionel Marsden, Cornelius O'Neill, Maggie Norden, Mark Hayes, Bruce Masefield, Susie Mutch, Edward Darley, Peter Dawson, Leona Curran, Josh Gibson and all at Vidal Sassoon, Dr Frances Corner at the London College of Fashion and, of course, Lisa Dyer and all at Carlton Books.

Picture Credits

The publishers would like to thank the following sources for their kind permission to reproduce the pictures in this book.

Key: t=Top, b=Bottom, c=Centre, l=Left and r=Right
Adams Picture Library: /John Adams: 136b, 137
©Bata Shoe Museum, Toronto (2008): 18, 19cl, 19r, 52, 123br, 140c&r, 184t&b
Bruno Magli: 119c, 127t, 148bl
Camera Press: 127cl, 132–3, 174t, 188l, 192cr
©Carlton Books: 83t&c, 127cr (Hand Beaded), 127bl&br

Corbis: /©Austrian Archives: 21, /©Michel Arnaud: 193br, /Bettmann: 12, 11l, 48, 78, 131t, 144tl, 145tl, 145br, 165, /©Barnabas Bosshart: 170tl, / Condé Nast archive: 4, 32tl, 41t, 49, 53, 56, 58, 60, 61, 67t, 79t, 81, 84t, 86t, 86bl&r, 88, 92–3, 94(Main), 96, 101, 104, 109, 110, 112tl, 113cl&cr, 118, 126, 129, 130, 135, 142, 143, 144br, 148, 149, 155tl, /Douglas Kirkland: 153, /Herb Schmitz: 162t, /Hulton-Deutsch Collection: 8cl, 10, 13r, 24r, 30, 33br, 40, 43, 55bl, 98–9, 136t, 171, /©David Lees: 100t, /©Massimo Listri: 69, 71b, 73br, /©Genevieve Naylor: 8r, 87t, 95, 113b, /©Philadelphia Museum of Art: 67b, /©Stefano Rellandini: 205tr, /©Steve Schapiro: 170br, /©Swim Ink 2, LLC: 47, /©Underwood & Underwood: 22, /©Pierre Vauthey/Sygma: 9cr, 151tr, 175t, 180tr, 180cr, 181
Getty: 8l&cr, 9cl, 17tl, 26bl, 27, 28tl, 33tr, 34tr, 35, 36, 37t&b, 38tl, 41b, 42tl, 44, 54tl, 59, 64–5, 77, 90t, 91, 102, 131bl, 139, 144tr, 145tr, 154, 201, 206bl, 210, /AFP: 191, 192tr, 206br, /f8 Imaging: 179t, /Popperfoto: 9l, 33l, 93tr, 116t, 134t, 156, /Time & Life Pictures: 70, 84b, 85, 98tl, 103t, 103b, 111, 112br, 123tl, 138, 157, 172, 190r, /Topical Press Agency; 14, /Roger Viollet: 46, /WireImage: 9r, 202t&b, 203, 204, 207
Courtesy Gina Shoes: 105, 106–7, 121, 160, 174b, 176, 177, 178, 193tl, 194, 198, 199, 212–3, endpapers
Collection of Kyoto Costume Institute, photo by Masayuki Hayashi: 186, 187bl&r
Magnum Photos: /Ferdinando Scianna: 187t
©Manolo Blahnik: 166, 167, 168, 169, 182tr, 183, 200
Mary Evans Picture Library: 16, 17tl, 24l, 26t, 42tr&br, 51, 54tr, 55tr, 63, 66, 73l, /Dryden Collection: 15t, /Illustrated London News: 23r, 25t, 39, / Vanessa Wagstaff Collection: 34tl
Musée international de la chaussure, Romans-sur-Iserè-France/ Christophe Villard: 45, 50, 62, 64tl, 64cl, 64bl&br, 65b, 90c&b, 94br, 108, 116b, 119l, 123tr&cr, 127cr (Gold), 132l, 145bl, 148br, 155tr, 155bl&br, 161, 175b, 179b, 180b, 182tl&bl, 188br, 192tr
Museo Salvatore Ferragamo: 68, 71t, 72, 73tr, 74, 75, 80tr, 100b, 131cr
Nicholas Kirkwood: 196
©Norman Parkinson Archive: 2–3, 82, 114, 117, 124, 125t, 128, 141, 146, 158, 164
Northampton Museum & Art Gallery; 15b, 19tl, 25b, 28cr, 29t&c, 34br, 54br, 55cl&br, 103c, 113t, 131br, 156br, 159bl&br, 163, 170tr, 171tl&tr, 182br, 189cb, 193tr, 193bl, 205cr&br
Redferns: 140l
Rex Features: /Bill Orchard: 120, /Mikko Oksanen: 150–1, /RESET: 205tl, /Sipa Press: 144bl, 190l, /Roger Viollet: 20, 97tl
Reuters: /Paolo Cocco: 1, /Chris Helgren: 209, /Philippe Wojazer: 197r
Terry de Havilland: 159tl, 197bl
Tod's: 193cl
Topfoto.co.uk: 122, 125b, 134b, 151br, 152bl
Victoria & Albert Museum: /V&A Images: 17b, 23l, 28bl, 29b, 33cr, 38r, 76l&r, 79b, 80bl, 83b, 87c&b, 97tr, 97cr&br, 98b, 119r, 133br, 152tl, 152br, 156c, 208
Vivienne Westwood: 162b, 189bl, 189br, 197tl
Walter Steiger: 185

Every effort has been made to acknowledge correctly and contact the source and/or copyright holder of each picture and Carlton Books Limited apologizes for any unintentional errors or omissions, which will be corrected in future editions of this book.

The publishers would especially like to thank the Kurdash family for access to the Gina Shoe collection and archive.